Wake Me From The NIGHTMARE

Advance Praise

"Want to help someone coping with grief following suicide (or any sudden, unexpected death)? Drop off a copy of this little book with a note saying, "Thinking of you with love". Get a copy for yourself too. This is a straightforward, simple guide to better understanding."

Steve Ahlgren, Lake Geneva, WI

"If you're struggling with grief from suicide or any other life changing loss, you will find strength and courage in the pages of this book. It's a heartfelt work from the heart of someone who has been there and a wonderful guide to understanding grief."

Kay Melson, Genoa City, WI

"I wish I'd had R. Jade McAuliffe's book about 20 years ago, when my sister took her own life. I was so busy 'being there' for my mother, I forgot how important it was to be there for myself.

From the very beginning, and throughout this book, I found many great quotes including this one: 'Partake in bodacious self-care practices.' But perhaps the most profound statement was found in her Conclusion: 'Death doesn't kill a relationship, it only alters it.' This is the best take-away statement I have ever read!"

Sharon Dexter, Lake Geneva, WI
Author of *I Will Not be Silent, Conversations with God, Seasons of My Soul*, and *A Call to Arms*
Find Sharon at her blog: www.singintosilence.blogspot.com
and at her website: www.godsfaithfulpromise.com

"While *Wake Me from the Nightmare* was written for those impacted by suicide loss, I think it should be required reading for everyone recovering from loss or trauma of any kind. Filled with stories from Jade McAuliffe's personal experiences and those of her clients, this book helps readers understand they are not alone, even the most 'out there' feelings and thoughts are normal, and real-world and 'out of this world' support is always available for the taking."

Melissa Drake, Los Angeles, CA
Intuitive Editor, Writer, and Coach.
Find Melissa at her website:
www.brillianttransformations.com
or email her at: collectivelybeneficial@gmail.com.

"This is a gem of a book not only for those struggling in some way with the effects of suicide but with any major loss. Jade writes with the deepest compassion and skill in coaching her readers through their own discovery and healing process in both a gentle and firmly supportive way. This book reads like Jade is sitting right next to you. Her words and her heart poured out on these pages mirror her struggle and the many gifts she's cultivated from it. Read along as she so passionately shares her wisdom and heart while sparking hope, courage and community."

Diane Burns, OTR/L, BCPP, RPT3 (Occupational Therapist, Board Certified Polarity Therapist, RYSE Practitioner and Teacher), Shrewsbury, MA, Holistic Healing, Gracepoint Holistic Health.
Find Diane at: www.gracepointholistichealth.com

"Suicide is one of life's major disasters. Jade shares her story and inspires you to heal your heart, body, and spirit as you remember the best of the person you loved. Thank you, Jade, for your beautiful book to help so many recovering from a devastating loss."

Linda Kroll, Chicago, IL, Therapist, Mediator, Attorney, and Chopra Certified Master Teacher of Meditation, Yoga, and Ayurveda. Author of *Compassionate Mediation® for Relationships at a Crossroad: How to Add Passion to Your Marriage or Compassion to Your Divorce*.
Find Linda at her website: www.LindaKroll.com.

"The loss of a loved one is a painful experience. Enduring the added trauma of loss to suicide makes this situation even more devastating. In this heartfelt and comforting book, Jade reminds you that you're not alone. She shares her own story, struggles, and realizations with honesty and compassion. The tools she offers are simple and essential in gently guiding the heartbroken through the journey of grief and mourning. Most importantly, Jade reminds us all that, ultimately, we're here to celebrate our loved ones (and ourselves) through a life well lived. This book is a must-have for anyone dealing with traumatic loss."

Virginia L'Bassi, Flying Vee Life Coaching, Sterling, MA
Find Virginia at: www.flyingveelifecoaching.com

"There is a sacred place within each of us where our deepest pain and our deepest love live. This book touches that place. Thank you, thank you for this powerful, profound experience."

Nancy J Early, CADC, Hoffman Estates, IL
Find Nancy at: 847-885-2676

"R. Jade McAuliffe pulls back the curtain on a culturally taboo topic and shines the light on suicide loss with such tenderness and grace. Her words are a balm to any aching heart grieving the sudden loss of a loved one. Being a suicide survivor myself, I know this messy, uncomfortable no-man's land that those left behind are forced to navigate. This is the book that lovingly and gently guides survivors through that desolate landscape. Having survived the sudden loss of both of her sisters, the author is a genuine authority on the topic and has transformed her own pain and journey into a practical process of healing, holding the reader's hand every step of the way. Thank you, Jade, for your courage to share your story and your wisdom to provide such a vital resource to those facing the heart-breaking grief of suicide loss."

Catherine S. Gregory, CMT, CMI, Boulder, CO, Founder of Fertile Being Healing and Author of *Fertile: The Wise Woman's Guide to Fertility Success* Find Catherine at: catherine@fertilebeing.com

"In my career of over two decades supporting thousands of survivors of abuse, trauma and cults to reduce physical, emotional, and money pain, I know the need for bringing support for trauma and suicide survivors out of the shadows and into day to day life. Thank you to the author of Wake Me from the Nightmare, R. Jade McAuliffe, for having the courage to survive, going to the depths she needs to, to bring this book to life while holding space for all of us who have been touched by suicide. Her courage alone brings hope, and this book can save the lives of the living."

Sofie Pirkle, Oakland, CA, Teacher, Bodywork Practitioner, Life Balance Consultant, 3rd Degree Black Belt & Master Instructor, Hand Analyst, Reiki Instructor, Transformation Catalyst Find Sofie at: www.thecultofsofie.com or 416-672-9872

"This new book, 'Wake Me from the Nightmare: Hope, Healing, and Empowerment After Suicide Loss,' belongs in every public library, as well as in all schools, and churches throughout the United States! It is an essential read for profession-als who counsel those who have attempted suicide, as well as for individuals trying to recover from the horrific suicide of a loved one. Book Clubs across our country will also become part of the healing team after discussing this groundbreaking work. The author eloquently lays out a process so redemptive, that shattered hearts can heal, and will ultimately be stronger in the broken places. Share the needed wisdom in this book with everyone you know, because eventually, we are all person-ally impacted by the unimaginable tragedy of suicide."

Mary Ann Moller-Gunderson, Lake Geneva, WI

"This book takes your hand and leads you through the darkest depths of your soul and back to the light. I would recom-mend it for anyone suffering the loss of a loved one."

Sheila Isaacs, Nashville, TN

"In 'Wake Me from the Nightmare,' R. Jade McAuliffe offers an empowering and creative process of healing from the grief of suicide. I found that the tools offered in her personal account were effective in transforming the intense and confusing pain of the many faces of grief. She does so in a way that enables the process to unfold, in its own unique way, by inviting us to heal our pain through the acceptance of our own hearts."

Marie Bigelow, Orange, MA

"In Wake Me from the Nightmare, R. Jade McAuliffe pas-sionately shares her grief, despair, and recovery to give hope to others who have experienced loss from suicide. She offers encouragement and, most importantly, provides specific coping strategies for support in this ongoing process!"

Mary Ann Decatur, Burlington, WI

"This book is a gift to the world and an in-depth masterpiece of understanding. The author beautifully and thoughtfully illustrates her own experiences and challenges dealing with loss, grief, and isolation. It leads the reader through these challenges and directly to the process of finding acceptance, peace, and healing. She explains in detail how to connect to the power that lives within while reminding us of our own uniqueness and connection to the Universe. This book is not only a story but also powerful resource for those searching for answers, support, peace, and healing. It is well written, easy to understand, and very inspiring. It is a guide to understanding not only suicide but also ourselves and our ability to find a path to our own healing. I highly recommend this book not only as a clinician but as a spiritual healer."

Katherine Skrzypek, Algonquin, IL, Life Coach, OFM, MFRT, Ph.D

Find Katherine at: katherineksk@yahoo.com

"This book offers a loving and personal account of what it's like to be a survivor of suicide loss. More importantly, it shares hope and help for others going through this nightmare. Read it and share it."

Maryann Udel, Los Angeles, CA, Founder of Sheltering Tree

"I became a survivor of suicide in 2005 and I wish this book would have been available to me then. I read every book Amazon had at the time. Most were comforting to know I was not alone, but they did not address the steps and exercises to go through the grieving process. I highly recommend this book to anyone who is clawing their way back to their new normal. The book will help you realize that it is okay to feel the way you do, exercises to deal with the guilt, the anger, the endless questions of why. I believe every survivor will benefit from reading this book and applying the step by step process to ensure that you not only will survive this tremendous loss, but you will be a stronger, healthier person when the sky begins to turn blue again."

Renay Elmore, Hattiesburg, MS

"This is a wonderful book! An easy read and hard to put down once you begin reading it! I believe it can be helpful for anyone experiencing the loss of a loved one, and not just a suicide loss. Jade's words are comforting. Her steps to recovery are easy to follow and practical! The best part about this book is knowing that Jade has personally experienced loss and grief, and she made it through stronger and happier than ever. Her experience adds empathy to the book. I highly recommend this book to anyone experiencing loss and grief."

Cathy Carroll, Northlake, IL

"I lost a loved one to suicide but not in the conventional sense. She drank herself to her death. I felt all the same feelings of despair and hopelessness R. Jade discusses in her book. I struggled with guilt, with shame, with loss. Reading this book opened my eyes to things I had been feeling but couldn't express or even admit to. Thank you, R. Jade for writing this and putting it out there for people to read, to open eyes to healing and feeling again. It's a process and it's not easy but it's so worth it in the end. To be able to breathe again, to laugh again, to live."

Elizabeth Harris, Racine, WI

"Author R. Jade McAuliffe walks alongside the reader by guiding them through suicide grief and sharing her personal experience. I know this book can help those who suffer due to complicated loss. I can confidently say this because it has already helped me. I used some of the suggested exercises to assist me with my own post-traumatic stress disorder (PTSD), and I found it effective and refreshing. I hope I never again have to see another suffer in pain due to suicide loss but, if I do, this book has provided more insight on how I might better address such a condolence. I pray this book will inspire others to find courage to live their best life, as it did me."

Shelley Salazar, Hoffman Estates, IL

"Astounding and powerful! R Jade McAuliffe bravely shares her story of surviving suicide loss. She gracefully offers the method that she used to regain control of her life! This book is a warm hug and a guide for people who feel like their life has collapsed from experiencing loss through the traumatic happenings of a suicide. In her book, Jade truly showcases as a heart of gold and a pillar of strength to lean on. I highly recommend!"

Ramses Rodriguez, Author of *What's Wrong with Me?*
Why Do I Panic?
Find Ramses at: ramsesrodriguez88@gmail.com

"I enjoyed this book so much. I love how the author was genuine and authentic as she shared her personal story of grief and recovery after suicide and trauma. Having experienced this in my life, I found each chapter confirmed and acknowledged the stages in the grief journey. The author gave the reader exercises, personal examples, and insight on how to deal with emotions, reactions from others, and how to get additional support. Her words were uplifting, encouraging and offered hope as we move through grief and step into healing. I would recommend this book to anyone experiencing loss and grief after someone they know has died to suicide."

Cara Williams, Henderson, KY

"A must have self-help book for grief, suicide loss and beyond! This is an invaluable tool for anyone grieving a suicide loss in their life. The author has blended a brilliant combination of helpful advice, from sharing her own personal story in a warm, reassuring and relatable way, to providing simple yet powerful self-healing exercises.

In my opinion this book isn't just for suicide loss survivors. I also find it to be a great resource for anyone grieving a traumatic loss or learning to heal from PTSD and related conditions.

Reading "Wake Me from the Nightmare" is like having your own personal cheerleader on your road to recovery. I found this book to be encouraging, comforting, and filled with hope for navigating such difficult circumstances in our lives."

Rebekah Ann Stephenson, MI, Poet, Artist and Miracle Hunter, living inspired.

Find Rebekah at: www.weliveinspired.com

"R. Jade is a great source of inspiration not only for people seeking solace in a time of heartbreak but to thrive in a season of change.

She has the power to support you to live with intention, learn your own truth and to not be afraid to speak it."

Megan Gillespie Jones, Charlottetown, PE, Canada

"R. Jade McAuliffe shares a deep and honest journey through the darkest times in her life. It was refreshing to learn that by surrendering to her deepest vulnerabilities in alignment with truly non-judgmental people she was able to leverage the strength needed to continue to purify her soul. This is a must read!"

Patrick Carragher, Red Bank, NJ

Wake Me *from the* NIGHTMARE

Hope, Healing, *and*
Empowerment After Suicide Loss

R. Jade McAuliffe

NEW YORK

LONDON • NASHVILLE • MELBOURNE • VANCOUVER

Wake Me from the Nightmare

Hope, Healing, and Empowerment After Suicide Loss

Published in New York, New York, by Morgan James Publishing in partnership
with Difference Press. Morgan James is a trademark of Morgan James, LLC. www.
MorganJamesPublishing.com

ISBN 9781642794137 paperback
ISBN 9781642794144 eBook
ISBN 9781642794151 audiobook
Library of Congress Control Number: 2018914663

Cover & Interior Design by:
Christopher Kirk
www.GFSstudio.com

Morgan James is a proud partner of Habitat for Humanity Peninsula
and Greater Williamsburg. Partners in building since 2006.

Get involved today! Visit
MorganJamesPublishing.com/giving-back

This is for my sisters.
Thank you for bringing me, and this book, to life.

Table of Contents

Foreword

Jade McAuliffe is a survivor.

How she lit a candle in the darkness of her life and became the woman she is today trumps any human interest story I've produced in 40 years as a sportswriter.

Jade is a healer of shattered souls.

Take it from me because she helped heal mine.

Allow me to briefly digress: In March 2015, I lost my beloved wife, Terri, on our 24th wedding anniversary. That was just 42 days after my older brother Greg unexpectedly died. To say the least, I was emotionally wrecked.

Spiritually taking me by the hand during that devastation was my friend, Elizabeth, who was my high school crush but eventually became a lifelong friend and pen pal from over 900 miles away.

In my lifetime, only my wife and mother meant more to me than Elizabeth, and she managed to soothe my broken heart during those difficult months after loss with reassuring and loving texts from the depths of her generous heart.

I needed Elizabeth's friendship at least as much as I needed oxygen during that time, as the cruelest of springs made way for a very lonely summer.

And it was destined to become even lonelier.

On a warm and fateful August morning, Elizabeth's husband contacted me with words that shattered my consciousness: Elizabeth was gone. She'd died to suicide.

Elizabeth left many loved ones behind, including her younger sister; a remarkable woman named Jade.

Jade and I arranged our first get together in September, one month to the day after losing Elizabeth. I was baffled by Elizabeth's exit and hoped Jade could offer some answers.

Other than passing references about Jade in letters from Elizabeth through the years, I knew nothing about her and had never even seen a photo.

But after five minutes of walking and talking together that sunny summer afternoon, Jade made me feel as though I'd known her most of my life.

She was warm and sensitive, and quickly became one of the most profound human beings I'd ever encountered.

Jade told me how the same despair that took her sister almost took her decades earlier. She told me about her broken relationships and about the pressure of raising four children alone.

She also told me how she was going to survive.

And she did more than survive.

My cherished friend has channeled a lifetime of energy into creating this magnificent volume of work for you, and she has done so while nearly single-handedly raising her children, who happen to love their mother dearly.

From the elegant prose of her eldest daughter to the scrawl of her youngest son, I've seen first-hand how much Jade's children adore her.

And just as I appreciate her for all she's done for me these last three years, I know you'll value her too.

Jade's friendship means the world to me.

I promise, this book will mean the world to you.

Peter Jackel

Sportswriter, The Journal Times

Welcome

I want to thank you for choosing this book and for finding the courage to acknowledge your heartbreak. This isn't easy when living within a society that teaches people to disconnect from themselves and others. A society which focuses on appearance, productivity, and status (none of which matter in the long run at all). We're trained early to hide our pain and post only stories of success and smiling faces instead. We're given pills to relieve discomforts when we're sick (but rarely do we ever find or resolve the issues which brought the illness on in the first place). We've unintentionally become an unconscious society of dodgers and pretenders, and we have a low tolerance for anything that gets in the way of our comforts and conveniences. We have a curious need for everything and everyone to look okay on the outside, so we can feel okay on the inside because on some level, *we're all running around freaking scared.*

As a society, we've forgotten who we are. But you haven't forgotten, and that's why you're here.

You are a survivor of suicide loss and a warrior of love.

You're here because your life, and the life of your lost loved one, *matters*. You're here because you know you need to find a way to deal with this devastation to be okay again. You're here to honor the longings of your broken heart. You're here because you're lost in a fog which you know can only be lifted with the help of others who've been there. You're here to learn how to *live* again because when your beloved took their life, they took yours along too. You're here because you're brave, and this doesn't mean you have to be strong. Let go, my friend. You don't always have to be strong. Here, you can show up any way you like. Please know always, that you, and your wide range of desperate, mixed-up, volatile, and beautiful feelings, will be accepted and honored too, *without conditions*. You and everything in you has a place here, and *it all matters*.

The world will try to tell you to move on before you're ready, but don't worry. This is your journey and you will determine your own timelines. The grieving process *won't* be rushed, and it *won't* be ignored either. It will prompt you. All you need to do is follow its lead and I promise you, you will be just fine. Yes, it will hurt, and yes, you will have to feel the feelings and do the actual work of grieving. I can't do that for you, but I *can* walk beside you. I can tell you it's going to be okay. I can understand you, validate you, reassure you, and honor you. I'm here for you, and I respect your journey. You can do this, and you will find hope and joy again.

Maybe sooner than you think.

In this book, I'll walk you through the process that honored me and my suicide grief.

It's simple and easy to follow. Everything I recommend to you can be done in your own unique way and in your own time. There's no need to rush through any of this. Healing traumatic grief is a lengthy process. It took me more than two and a half years to really clear my head and feel solid again, so please be gentle with yourself. This is a marathon, not a sprint. Take the lessons in small doses, and don't do more than your body allows. Trying to do too much at once will drain your energy reserves.

It's going to be tough enough to get through the day and stay on top of whatever responsibilities are required of you right now. Keep these responsibilities to the lowest possible minimum. You're going to need lots of time to rest, grieve, and regroup. This alone is a full-time job and you can expect to tire more easily.

You can also expect any number of physical symptoms to appear along the way (these always correlate to emotions). Don't be afraid to check with your medical doctor or naturopath if any pains or symptoms become problematic. It never hurts to be sure there isn't something else brewing.

Expect your emotions to be all over the spectrum. This is normal, and often unpredictable. Be honest with your friends, loved ones, and kids regarding what you can and can't handle right now, and don't take on any heavy commitments. Now is the time to focus on you and your needs, not everyone else's. You won't have the brain space or the energy for this now. If you have young kids, assemble all the help you can so you can have blocks of time to yourself. If you can get away for an occasional long weekend alone, that works too. Do whatever you can with what you have. Even short breaks are better than none. You will stumble, and you will fall. I know I did, but like anything else, following your grief waves will be a practice, and one which won't be perfect.

I didn't grieve perfectly, but I did grieve effectively.

My personal success was the result of acting consciously and intentionally rather than pretending to be strong and together. (Which was, by the way, my default presence. Thank you, American media.) In all honesty, this happened partly because I was too tired and despaired to pretend. My strength was gone. What I had instead was a deep rage, which would no longer be silenced, and this was the emotion dying to be heard. It refused to stay quiet to comply with society's rules. This was the voice of my spunky inner child (later referred to as my Inner Healer) and she had a lot to say about pretending. It was she who woke me from my nightmare, and I've been following her lead ever since.

The good news is we all have an Inner Healer.

Their voices have just been drowned out by the noise, busyness, and the oppressive rules of society, but we don't have to be distracted anymore. This is the perfect time to begin listening and creating your *own rules* for living and loving (and everything else). I will teach you how to connect to your inner power, so you can begin to deeply heal and *thrive*. There really is life after suicide loss and, although it will be different, it will have your name written all over it. A new life is waiting, and hand in hand, we'll find our way together.

CHAPTER 1:

No Man's Land

Suicide loss broke you. It pushed you out of your old life and into the center of the unknown. You're shocked, terrified, angry, and confused. You might be afraid to open your eyes in the morning. You might be scared to leave your house. The world as you once knew it changed with a single decision. You're devastated and heartbroken. You and your life will never be the same.

I know you've been shattered and left to pick up the pieces.

I know you're living in a nightmare of shock, disbelief, and despair.

I know you're questioning how you'll ever survive the pain.

I know you're barely breathing and it's all you can do to get out of bed every morning.

I know your sobs are so deep you think your heart might explode.

I know safety and predictability have been replaced by terror, panic, and anxiety.

I know the pain in your chest is your heart's desperate protest to hang on when it's forced to let go.

And I know you're blaming yourself...

but it wasn't your fault. I promise you, *it wasn't your fault.*

I know this because I lost my sister Elizabeth to suicide and survived two suicide attempts of my own in the late 1990s. I'm not proud of this fact, but it does give me a different perspective. I offer my experience to shed some light onto the darkness of yours.

Suicide is a solitary act. It's also, very often, an impulsive one.

Even if you *knew* your loved one was struggling with a troubling life event, illness, depression, or other mental illness, there was no way to monitor their every move. There was no way to ensure their safety, to be certain that they were taking their medicine as prescribed, or that they were having productive conversations about what was bothering them.

Their suicide wasn't *your* choice. It was *theirs.*

Despite everything we *can* control, we can't control the beliefs or actions of *others.*

Believe me when I tell you their suicide likely wasn't the result of a single event. Hopelessness tends to build over time, as does the exhaustion which accompanies the fight to stay alive, and there's no way to ever know the secret life that exists between a person's ears. You can drive yourself to the brink of insanity trying to figure it out.

They likely couldn't express the depth of their pain and believed there were no other options. I know that place: the place of exhaustion, emptiness, and desperation. The truth is by ending their own pain, they only passed it on to you, and you're the one left to clean up the mess. You have every right to question, rage, and recoil. It isn't fair, and you don't deserve this. It might even feel like a punishment, and your rage is justified. I pray you will give yourself permission to *feel it all.* The good, the bad, and the ugly. Every feeling has a purpose and you're allowed to experience them all in your own way.

After suicide loss, there's a natural need to blame. When we're trying desperately to make sense of a desperate act, it's normal to want to know *why* it happened or *what* made someone choose death over life. When pieces are missing from any story, the brain automatically tries to fill in the gaps. (That's its job.) Unfortunately, people are complex and the answers for why and what might never be known. This is a scary and desperate place. This *not* knowing can be excruciating, making you feel as though you and your life are hanging in the balance. And there are always more questions: Why couldn't I help her? Why wouldn't she talk to me? Why didn't I know how desperate she was? It's easy to get lost in this black hole of despair. Crushed, raw, and confused, you're left to navigate the wreckage of your current reality and what will now never be. It's a slippery slope, and I recommend offering yourself a little grace right off the bat. Release your need to know the answers to all the whys. One day you *will* know, and the answers might surprise you. Things are seldom as they seem on the surface. The longer I live, the more I wake up to this reality.

The Cost of Grieving Alone

Above all else, I want you to know you aren't alone. I'm here to assure you: Surviving suicide loss *is* possible. You can, and you will, eventually find equilibrium again, but you need to reach out for support as soon as possible. There's no time to lose, because an irreplaceable life is at stake: yours.

I want you to take this very seriously. Suicide grief is messy and complex.

Many feel they can't or "shouldn't" share their burden with others because it's too heavy, even for them. They fear judgment, shame, and blame. After all, if they're having trouble comprehending and carrying this load, how will anyone else be able to deal with it? Trust me when I tell you, though, that silence can be deadly. It serves no one and, in the end, *hurts everyone.* You're currently sorting through this wreckage, and it's time to end the cycle, not only for your sake, but for the sake of your entire family. The risk of suicidality rises in family members who have suffered a suicide loss or have family that made suicide attempts. Survival is serious business. Don't risk becoming another statistic. Know, above all else, whatever you're feeling is normal and needs to be expressed.

The fact is, it takes a small army to successfully navigate the unpredictable storms of complicated grief. (Never underestimate the power of numbers. If one person should tire, another can step in.) Just be sure to choose carefully, and know you'll be better able to weather the waves when you assemble adequate supports early on.

"One of the realities of grief and loss is that the rest of the world seems to keep on going forward, while we feel like we've been stopped in our tracks."
– Alan Wolfelt

Something seems amiss when life marches on as usual after a loss.

I wondered why the sun shined so brightly the day of my sister's funeral. Didn't God know He was supposed to deliver raging thunderstorms that day? Hail? Damaging winds? It wasn't supposed to be *sunny*! That made it seem like any other day. The world didn't seem to notice or care that my sister was gone, and while I knew she was in a better place, it didn't seem that God cared either.

Knowing I'd lost my oldest sister, Sue, nineteen years earlier, a friend of Elizabeth's mentioned at the memorial that I might want to solicit outside support to deal with my second tragedy. That was my plan, but I knew I'd better follow through because the universe always speaks through others. (My faith might've been shaken, but it wasn't completely gone.) I also knew I had long history of anxiety and depression. I couldn't afford *not* to get help, and I don't doubt for a moment that my supports saved my life.

Yes, I'd been through loss before, but Elizabeth was alive when Sue died, and we were able to help each other through that pain. As sisters, we also had each other's stories along with mutual memories between us to keep her alive. That in and of itself helped us to heal faster. There is always strength in numbers. This time, though, I was alone.

Nothing in the world could've prepared me for facing this experience again on my own. Both of my sisters were dead, and I felt like an orphan: lost, confused, and empty. Suddenly I was eight years old again, in their closet hiding from the monsters.

Grief offered me no mercy. It hit *hard*, waking me up to my nightmare each morning with the inevitable light of day. I only felt safe in the dark sanctuary of my bedroom and, even then, I couldn't sleep. It hurt too much. I hurt too much.

People who haven't experienced suicide loss often fight to understand it. Their well-intentioned questions and comments can come off as callous, trite, or downright insensitive. Unfortunately, suicide and mental illness continue to be stigmatized and met with judgment by an unwitting society. It's hard to believe but, even today, some religions teach that those who complete suicide end up in hell. Stay as far away from these people as possible. These beliefs will only derail you and your delicate process.

Someone close to me once mentioned that, "We could forgive [my] sister because God had probably forgiven her." Probably? And for what, exactly? Making an emotionally loaded, split-second decision based on the distorted beliefs she bought into that day? People do that all the time! The only difference is most don't end up dead as a result. No, I don't believe for a moment God judges anyone based on decisions made from confusion and brokenness. He knows the heart, and He cares for the broken.

The world can be cold, but it's only due to fear and confusion. Unfortunately, that's not much consolation when you're in the throes of grief. There will be people who avoid you because they won't know what to say or how to act. Give them the benefit of the doubt if you can and lean in to the ones who find a way to understand. Above all else, follow your gut, and know you don't *ever* have to abide by anyone else's timelines. Grief has its own timeline, and it isn't "Be Healed in 30 Days or Less." Grief is a marathon, never a sprint. The world might want you to "hurry up and get over it," but your heart is begging you to slow down, listen in, and ask for help. Please take heed. It knows exactly what it needs.

My Wish for You

I wanted to write this book to speak my truth: Grief is only love in another form. It's the process of letting go of the *body*, but not of the relationship. Your loved one lives on... in your heart, your mind, and your soul. You are inextricably connected. Your beloved can be as close or as far away as you wish. You get to decide. You are in charge now.

This is your sacred time to grieve what was and to figure out what you want for your future. I pray you'll choose to become your own best friend, advocate, and lie detector. I hope you'll forget about other people's preconceived notions about who you are and who you should be and learn to stand firm in what you know for sure. Yourself.

I know you're shaken and you're scared. You're wondering if you'll ever be okay again. You might be questioning everything and everyone you thought you knew. I know I did. What I didn't realize was I knew myself and my situation better than I initially believed. Things aren't always as they appear on the surface, and the truth has a way of revealing itself, in time. It must reveal itself. It's the universal law.

You will get through this, and you won't have to do it alone. I'll teach you what I've learned about love, loss, and life, and together, we'll find a way back to normalcy.

For now, please know it's enough just to *be*. *You* are enough, and you're right where you need to be. Put one foot in front of the other and keep on walking. Breathe. Do only what you need to do, and then do the next thing. I know you're terrified. I know it's taking every ounce of strength you have just to survive the day. I know the unbearable weight of your loneliness, and I'm familiar with the gaping void of emptiness. I've been there and back. But you can do this. Together, we can do this. I've got your back.

> Will you return to hold my hand
> I need your strength to understand
> 'cause my heart aches with words unsaid
> racing through my troubled head
> I long to hear your quiet voice
> and laughter...
> but it's not a choice

Few know about the bond we share
and how you helped to fuse the tear
you validated what I knew
the same truth that tormented you
This loss has left a gaping hole
but it can't kill your ardent soul
You still live on to teach and guide
and help me from the other side
I'll stay strong to shine our light
until it's time to reunite
and love will find a way to mend
this brokenness inside... again

CHAPTER 2

My Story

I was the youngest of four siblings, with a six-year gap between myself and my brother. I didn't enjoy being referred to as "the baby" of the family (a title which I allowed to define me well into my thirties) but I loved having people to look up to, and my sisters quickly became my biggest influencers. There were eight years between myself and Elizabeth, and nine between me and my oldest sister, Suzanne. They shared a bedroom and I had my own, but I spent as much time in theirs as possible which, looking back, probably drove them crazy.

I am a highly sensitive and intuitive person, and I learned early on these qualities often left others annoyed and uncomfortable. I was born an agitator and within a chaotic and dysfunctional family, this was not an admirable quality. As an emotional big mouth, few things went unacknowledged by me. I was constantly asking questions and challenging the status quo. This resulted in often being left out of the loop of general information, which only added insult to injury, making my quest for knowledge more insistent. This wasn't appreciated, and I spent a lot of time alone. Looking back, I think we all did.

In school I got along fine until about the third grade, when I had to leave the public school in exchange for a parochial education. Things started out okay, but the kids soon discovered my sensitivities and insecurities. I became an easy target for bullies. I fought back (often in downright dirty ways) but this only made my misery escalate. I was desperate to fit in *somewhere,* but school never became that place for me. The harder I tried to belong, the more I found myself alone. I didn't fit in anywhere.

At nine, I decided if I looked differently, people might like me more. I became bulimic and spent most of my days frantically exercising, trying to lose the ten pounds I believed were holding me back from the good life. I never lost the weight, and I still couldn't keep my emotions in check. I was a wreck, and I felt like a complete failure. No matter how hard I tried in school, I had a solid B minus average. I would never look like the other girls. (I looked more like an athletic boy, and strangers often referred to me as "young man." My dad found this funny and reassured me that, at sixteen, I'd be able to validate my gender by lifting my shirt. Wrong again. Thanks, Dad.)

More than anything, I wanted to be cool like my sisters.

To me, they seemed to have it all together. Really, none of us had it together. We were all just trying to survive. Some did this more gracefully than others, winning a few accolades along the way, but none of us got by unscathed. I was *not* graceful, and my downward fall was steady and consistent. I'm certain I was clinically depressed by the age of eight, and by the time I was eighteen, my bulimia was totally out of control. I dropped out of college and was throwing up so often, I didn't feel much of anything anymore. I'd found the perfect way to numb everything: the pain, my body, and the memories. Until the flashbacks started. Then, I became completely unglued.

I ended up hospitalized several times to control the bulimia and depression.

On the road to mental health, I've been diagnosed with a multitude of mental illnesses including Major Depressive Disorder, PTSD, C-PTSD, bulimia, anorexia, OCD, and Generalized Anxiety Disorder. I've been on anti-psychotics and other medications used to treat Bipolar Disorder because antidepressants alone didn't offer enough relief. (This is common protocol for trauma patients.) As my anxiety escalated, I was unable to sleep or function without taking high doses of anti-anxiety and sleep medications. My treatment team finally decided I wouldn't survive if I didn't emancipate, so my legal address became the hospital's until they were able to secure me a residence in a local group home. In the meantime, I lived in a halfway house on the hospital grounds.

About four months after moving into the new group home, I fell in love, moved in with my fiancé, and got a job. We married at the tail end of that same year, and life began looking up. We had two beautiful babies together, but the flashbacks and nightmares became relentless. I suffered from panic attacks and insomnia and couldn't stand to be touched.

We stopped talking, slept in separate rooms, and continued to grow further and further apart.

Again (although I was equally responsible for the demise of our marriage) I felt alienated, rejected, and inherently flawed. I believed my family deserved better and that I was nothing but a burden and a drain. My children needed a happy mother who could provide them comfort and security, and my husband needed a partner he could count on. I was a train wreck, and decidedly neither. I made two attempts at my life within a year. My husband, in an act of desperation (and legitimate anger), had me committed to a mental hospital after my second attempt, and I finally decided enough was enough. God obviously wanted me *here,* so I needed to find a way to stay. This meant leaving my home and finding a new treatment team. I needed to get myself back together or I would be no good for anyone. I needed to work with people who specialized in trauma, understood my history, and could help manage my symptoms without over-medicating me.

I applied for disability right away and hired new supports.

About four months later, just before Christmas, the phone rang in the middle of the night. It was my sister Elizabeth, and she was frantic. "Sue had a heart attack!" "What?" I panicked. I'd just seen her the month before! I tried to get details, but Elizabeth was too upset. I immediately called my parents' house and my dad said it wasn't a heart attack. Sue was found unresponsive in her bed but was now at the hospital and being monitored. He seemed hopeful, so I went back to sleep relieved that it wasn't a heart attack and assured she was in the right place. I knew when the phone rang at five a.m., though, she was gone.

My husband answered the phone as I closed my eyes. I walked into the living room. He said the words, "Your sister passed away." I broke down and hugged him. Then, I instantly thought of my mother. She had to be devastated. I needed to go to her. She would need me to be strong. So, I was.

The next several days were a blur, as we traveled west to be with my sister's husband and three kids. We were all in shock. The kids were young, aged seven to fifteen. I felt helpless in my attempts to console them, but I was grateful for the time we'd spent together over the past year. It was unusual for me to have the opportunity to visit with them more than once every year or two, and that year, I made three trips.

I was there to witness a notable decline in Sue's health. She was in a frightening amount of pain and obviously depressed. She insisted on forging through her housework, every day past midnight, and she would sleep during the day, often until noon.

One day, I found her lying face down and sideways across her bed. This was not normal.

The sparkle in her eyes disappeared and she engaged in conversation less and less. I begged her to rest and helped her in any way I could, but she was driven and stubborn and her home had to be perfect. (Stubbornness and perfectionism ran deep in all of us.)

Elizabeth often remarked that Sue's cleaning obsession reached unhealthy levels when she resorted to wall washing, and there was no doubt anyone could safely eat her deliciously crafted four course meals from her kitchen floor. It was always that clean.

Her home was her castle and she took pride in keeping it beautiful. It was her greatest desire to make her guests feel comfortable and welcomed, and we always were.

In her efforts to care for everyone else, though, she never really took care of herself. It was heartbreaking to watch her suffer in silence. During my last visit, I caught her crying in her bedroom while listening to Celine Dion's "Because You Loved Me." I asked what was wrong, but she wouldn't answer. Looking back, I'm not sure I'd ever seen her break down before. I'd only ever seen her cry a single tear or two accompanied by a far-away stare. Her pain was heartbreaking to witness.

There is no more helpless a feeling than not being able to reach someone when you know they're hurting. When you recognize that look of utter exhaustion and emptiness. It's as if the body is present but the will has checked out. That's what hopelessness looks like, and it's terrifying.

Ultimately, Sue's death was determined "accidental." At the time, reading that word in the autopsy report was a comfort. Now, after recent events, that determination has become more of a question for me. One day it will be clarified and, until then, I will rest in the knowing that her energetic presence is still alive and always very, very near.

Four months after Sue's death, I received my first disability payments.

I moved into a cheap studio apartment in a nice neighborhood. My husband and I eventually divorced, but we co-parented as best we could. Within three years, I got a full-time job which got me off disability and back on my feet. My recovery was far from perfect, but it was steady, and over the years, my traditional Western mental health care regimen gradually morphed into more of an unconventional spiritual journey. I eventually started a cleaning business, so I could be around for my kids, and I married (and divorced) again. I was also blessed with two more kids.

In 2004, I bought my first house.

I quickly became immersed in weekend rehab projects, and learned to replace sinks, faucets, and toilets. I replaced my kitchen floor, refinished the cabinets, and painted my entire house. I surprised myself every weekend, and my kids were impressed with the cosmetic changes. Somehow, there was always food on the table and enough money to pay the mortgage but, I wasn't entirely satisfied. I was still wrangling with the residual effects of my trauma and struggling to understand and break free from the programs that ran me.

I often felt "less than" for not finishing school (even though I had no desire to obtain a specific degree), and often felt a deep sense of shame for not doing "more" with my life. Although I was a responsible and successful single parent, these thoughts consumed me more than I care to mention. I had many interests and dreams, but never made time to pursue them. Instead, I kept myself busy with a never-ending list of mundane chores while *Gilmore Girls* episodes played in the background. (Hey, if you're going to zone out, you might as well be subconsciously influenced by a strong female lead. Love her or hate her, Lorelei Gilmore was funny, witty, and lived life on her own terms.) I lost nearly ten years in this loop, but it helped me through some difficult times. Sometimes, all you do is survive, and I knew how to do that.

When the phone rang at 6:30 on a warm August morning, I knew it wasn't going to be good news, but nothing could've prepared me for what I was about to hear. My sister Elizabeth was gone. She'd taken her life the afternoon before. I remember hanging up the phone feeling sick, shocked, and furious. I started to shake. As I sat in disbelief, something inside of me snapped. I was jolted out of a deep sleep and forced to wake up. I was disoriented, but fully conscious. From that moment on, I could no longer pretend everything was okay. I wouldn't. I couldn't. I was heartbroken, and my life would never be the same. I'd lost my last living sister, surrogate mother, mentor, protector, and fearless advocate. I was terrified and felt utterly and completely orphaned.

Elizabeth was the wise, responsible one. The strong one. The one who, managed to maintain focus and dive headfirst into every one of her goals, including a master's degree, athletic notoriety, a full and active social life, and, eventually, a beautiful family. She had it all. She was humble and kind, and I deeply admired her. She was the family go-to. Within any crisis, she was there with easy answers, making the rest of us look like life amateurs which, indeed, we were.

Our bond was one of the earliest and most important of my lifetime. It was the impetus for all I've been able to accomplish and, from it, came the strength and wisdom that helped me to survive.

Her six-year battle with mental illness created the sense of urgency I needed to put together the broken pieces that hid inside all of us. Her memories revealed themselves at random times and eventually manifested into debilitating anxiety and depression, leaving her unable to function. It looked, to me, like a classic case of C-PTSD. We had very similar struggles. So similar, it was spooky.

The Matter of Life and Death

When the puzzle started coming together for me, I didn't want to accept it, but Elizabeth's suicide removed all remaining doubt, and I knew my days would be numbered if I didn't find a way to make some sort of peace with the past. Every one of us attempted to end the pain at some point, and upon this realization, I became deeply concerned for my own well-being. I'd never really given myself permission to come first in my own life, and this had to change *immediately*.

I decided my grief journey was sacred and that nothing (and no one) would stop me from my right to process this unbearable loss in a deeply authentic way. I'd already lost Sue. Not Elizabeth too. It was more than I could handle. This was my wake-up call. Little did I know my entire life was about to change.

My Awakening

I was talking about suicide the day Elizabeth took her life.

I don't recall how, but I do remember my client speaking about a close friend who was battling depression and suicidal ideation. I don't remember mentioning my sister, but I do recall the final words I uttered on the subject that day... "I've been in that desperate place, and I could never blame anyone for wanting to end that kind of torment."

Those words will probably haunt me until I'm dead.

It makes sense in retrospect. Although we hadn't been emotionally or physically close in years, my sister and I had a very strong energetic connection. My body knew she'd left before my brain found out. I still shudder when I think back to that afternoon and wonder if I'd only supported her better or tried harder to connect, she'd still be here today.

The silence in Elizabeth's home became an unexpected comfort to me during the days following her passing. The time I spent there helped me to reconnect to the love and gentle light that was always her energetic core. I don't know how to adequately explain the healing that took place during that tender time. It was the stillness. I could feel her in the stillness.

When I returned home after the memorial, I attempted to get back to work and to life as I had always known it but instead, noticed my own dysfunction: The way I kept quiet when I had something to say. The way I held myself back from doing the things I said I'd always wanted to do. When did I shut down and where did I go?

I was waking up out of a thirty-year slumber and realizing the life I was leading no longer made sense to me. I had been hiding for years; behind my sister, behind my kids, and even behind my husbands. I finally saw the ugly truth. *I was living a lie.*

Somehow, I managed to cram myself into a tiny closet behind a mountain of random stuff, and none of it belonged to *me*. What I had been doing, how I had been behaving, and even what I had been *wearing* suddenly didn't make sense anymore. It wasn't *me*.

I remember sitting on my bed, shaking my head and wailing, "Oh my God. They're both *gone*. The two people in my life who *helped me* to survive my pain *didn't survive their own*."

Was it possible that the decades I spent emoting, questioning, and yapping *kept me alive*? I was always considered the "emotional disaster" of the family. I was labeled the "sick" one. (But I wasn't alone. We each held that title at one point or another.) I sat completely stunned with this "new" revelation and woke up to the truth of who I *really* was. I knew I needed to start *living* again, and I wasn't about to wait for permission to follow my dreams. It was time to give it to *myself.*

No more would I wait or hold myself back out of fear because I might fail, or because something might not work out as I'd planned. My days of waiting were over. If I was going to fail, at least I'd know I tried. There was no time to lose and I wouldn't stay small anymore.

I created a list of things I'd always wanted to do but didn't because of lack (lack of energy, lack of time, lack of money, lack of courage, lack of support) and then I got busy.

I turned back to books and poetry and began tapping into more creative forms of expression. My daughter loaned me a book called *Prosperity Pie: How to Relax About Money and Everything Else*, by an author who calls herself SARK. I read it in two days, and then found a six-month online webinar called "Manifesting Your Succulent Wild Life," created and led by the same inspirational author. I felt myself coming back to life.

Within the online group, I was granted access to some of the most powerful, creative, and courageous women I have ever known! I learned quickly that I could *grieve and live at the same time*. Together, we took a brave (and sometimes dark) dive into some serious self-introspection.

We learned how to manage the voices of our inner critics and re-establish our personal boundaries. We connected to our inner wisdom and cared for our own feelings. We learned how to break down large, ominous projects into fun and attainable bite-sized wins. We cared for ourselves in big ways while exploring our problematic relational patterns. We learned how our early programming taught us how we related to money and we learned how to set ourselves free from those scarcity mindsets. We cared for our inner kids and we cared for each other.

It was emotional, liberating, fun, and exactly what I needed to survive the coming turbulent months. Things were changing fast, and I wasn't about to hinder the process. I committed to change, no matter what it took.

I learned to trust myself again. I was no longer hiding or wishing or waiting. I was *doing*.

I found myself through the unconditional kindness and support of women who had struggled and conquered and were traveling the same path: back to themselves.

I would give anything to have my sisters here with me now, physically cheering on my efforts, but there is one thing I know for sure: I am never alone.

Your Life Is Calling

Suicide loss shakes you to the core, but your grief can lead you back to peace and sanity if you're willing to follow its lead. It wants to help you, and so do I. It won't be an easy journey, but it will be a meaningful one. Know that there *will* be obstacles. Exhaustion, PTSD, and depression are common roadblocks for suicide loss survivors. I want you to know, too, that disorientation, confusion, and suicidal thoughts might surface during this process. While this is normal, these thoughts should *never* be discounted or taken lightly. It is of utmost importance to be as transparent as possible with your support system throughout this healing journey. You owe it to yourself and to your remaining loved ones. The National Suicide Prevention Lifeline is available 24/7 (800-273-8255) should you need an empathetic ear. They know how to help in times of crisis. You can also use the Crisis Text Line by texting "hello" to 741741 (also available 24/7). Please don't try to tough it out. People are waiting to support you.

My process helped me, and it will help you navigate *whatever* feelings come your way. All of them are normal and need to be welcomed. There is no such thing as a negative feeling. We need to embrace them all to heal.

I know you want relief, and the only way out of this nightmare is to walk gently and carefully into the storm. Don't worry … I'm willing to hold your hand. Your new life is patiently waiting on the other side of this, and you can go as slowly as you need to, but please, please keep going. I've got you.

CHAPTER 3

The Process of Awakening

"There is a sacredness in tears. They are not the mark
of weakness, but of power. They speak more eloquently
than ten thousand tongues. They are the messengers
of overwhelming grief, of deep contrition, and of
unspeakable love."
– Washington Irving

I know you want an end to your pain.
I know you wish you would wake up to realize it was all just a horrible nightmare. You'd be able to get on with life as you knew it before any of this happened. You knew who you were then. Now you're not sure about anything. You died the day your loved one did, and there is no "getting back to normal." Your life and world flipped upside down. Nothing feels good, predictable, or safe.

This is a frightening place: the space between what was and what will be. Who will you be now? What will you do with the raging emotions? Maybe you aren't even feeling anything because you're still in shock. There is no one right way to feel and process your grief. But you do have to find a way to work through it or your own life will be in jeopardy.

The world won't hold your grief space for long. It (and others close to you) might expect you to move through the process faster than you're able because it makes them feel uncomfortable and helpless. But don't worry about them. This time, you need to put *yourself* and *your* needs first. Facing your grief head-on will require every ounce of strength you can muster... but that is precisely what will get you through this horrific experience.

Many people choose to push their feelings down for fear of becoming too burdensome for others. Don't get caught in this trap. It will only slow you down and delay your healing. You deserve a full and complete recovery, and you deserve honor and respect as you brave this process. If you leave your grief behind too soon, it will find a way to be heard and acknowledged later (and at the least convenient times). Mourning is not for sissies, and many are too afraid to do it because it *hurts*. But what's more painful? Following the pain *as* you're mourning, or dealing with uncontrollable fits of rage, depression, and PTSD later? If you can give yourself permission to deal with it now, you'll be less likely to turn to things on the outside to soothe you (food, alcohol, drugs, shopping, sex, insert your numbing drug of choice here).

Know that your best advice will always come from *inside,* and not from the outside.

Your body will tell you what it needs to heal. If you can learn to listen closely and follow its lead, everything else will fall into place. Conscious grieving *will* heal your suicide loss. It healed mine.

This probably sounds too simple, but simple is best when dealing with suicide grief.

You have enough to deal with now. Let's concentrate on the basics so you can follow your body to your own AWAKENING process.

I discovered the nine-step AWAKENING process as I navigated my own suicide loss, and I believe it saved my life.

It's too easy to drop into the black hole of isolation, hopelessness, and despair.

PTSD, depression, and suicidality are real threats to suicide loss survivors, but honoring the sacredness of your journey is key toward accepting and dealing with the enormity of your loss. Grief is merely love in disguise. This book will walk you through this truth and back into peace and understanding.

A – Assemble Supports

We're not meant to do this alone. Surround yourself with supportive, nonjudgmental people. It's okay to ask for help.

W – Walk Gently into Your Process

The grieving process can't be rushed. Small, gentle steps lead to sustainable healing and integration. Giving yourself permission to grieve in your own time is a huge gift.

A – Align with Your Inner Healer

You can't heal if you don't feel safe. Your Inner Healer knows how to move you through grief effectively. When you can hear and connect to the wisdom of your Inner Healer, you always know the "next right step."

K – Know and Speak Your Truth

Being real about how you feel will make you less likely to get "stuck" in the bonds of hopelessness, depression, and despair. Wholehearted mourning means *holding back nothing*. As we give ourselves permission to "be where we are," we release resistance to facing difficult feelings.

E – Emotions are Necessary

No, you're not crazy! Feeling, accepting, and letting them go is one of the most painful and necessary parts of the grieving process. In this chapter, you'll receive some tips and tricks to managing some of the most difficult and bothersome emotions.

N – Nurture Yourself

When you're empty, you need to fill up again. Time connecting to spirituality, nature, and creativity can soothe and restore your weary body and mind. Naps and other self-care practices will ensure your ability to go the distance.

I – Invoke the Sacred Connection

Death might end a physical life, but not a relationship. Your loved one lives on, and you can keep that connection open. Create space for communication and watch for the signs.

N – Navigate the New

Who are you *really*? What would you like to be doing? What if you stopped waiting and started doing it right now, slowly and imperfectly (with support)? Did you know creating new experiences can break negative patterns and help rewire your brain to create more positive results? I can teach you how.

G – Going Forward in Faith

No, there's no getting over the loss of your loved one, but letting go doesn't mean you'll forget them, either. You'll just find a little more peace in dealing with their absence. You'll realize their death was not your fault. It was their choice.

The AWAKENING process is slow and simple.

It's a process of becoming aware and taking conscious and deliberate action every day. It's about listening in and showing up for yourself and your grief in an authentic way. It's about owning your experience and allowing what is. This isn't anybody else's journey. It's *yours*. Claim your space. *Express your love*. It's the greatest gift you'll ever give to yourself *or* your loved one.

CHAPTER 4

Assemble Supports

"The friend who can be silent with us in a moment of despair or confusion, who can stay with us in an hour of grief and bereavement, who can tolerate not knowing … not healing, not curing, that is a friend that cares."
– Henri Nouwen

A s human beings, we're designed for connection. We aren't meant to do life alone. We need the comfort of others to heal from devastating loss. To begin integrating our grief, it's necessary to allow others to listen to *and* validate it. This does not mean, however, that it's ever okay for others to try to "fix" it (or us). We and our grief, although learning to coexist, are fine just as we are and exactly *where* we are.

No Judgments Please

I want to be very clear when I suggest that you find supports who are open, compassionate, and nonjudgmental. The last thing you need right now is to take on anyone else's feelings regarding *your* situation. This can be tricky, especially if you're prone toward codependency, or are connected to people who buy into the stigma of suicide itself.

These people will have their own opinions regarding you, your lost loved one, and your recovery process, but those opinions are none of your business.

Don't take them on. They have no idea how you're feeling or what you're going through (and they're probably happier not knowing). Please don't allow their limitations to influence the way you think or feel about yourself. They might mean well, but people like this will only poison your process.

Above all, be *honest* and *real* – and *be* with people who are honest and real.

Don't get caught in the trap of minimizing your feelings or needs to make your appearance more palatable for others. This only undermines your process and puts you in caretaker mode. This is both unkind and unfair to your broken heart, which desperately needs unconditional love and acceptance right now. Your job, at this moment, is to care for *yourself* (and your kids if you have them). This, after all, is *your* sacred journey.

It's best to have three to five supports dedicated to sticking with you through this process without trying to hurry, guilt, or shame you. If you're at all wondering where they stand, just ask them. Let them *show* you who they are. Don't rely on words alone because words without action are meaningless. I have a feeling you already know who in your life is safe, but people can and will surprise you.

It's important to know the person you're most counting on might not be the one who sees you through this. This can be a tough lesson, but it's still better to learn the truth about who you can and can't count on in difficult times sooner rather than later. People have baggage, and if they haven't dealt with their own stuff, they certainly won't be able to help you carry or unload yours. It's not their fault, it's just where they're at on their own journey.

It can be wise to hire a professional counselor or coach for additional support. It was a huge relief for me just *knowing* I had someone I could share with on a regular basis: someone with my best interests in mind who would help me weather the storm of my emotions or simply hold space for my grief. Everyone needs a witness, and everyone deserves one. Pastoral counselors can be wonderful choices during this time, if their focus is on God's *love*, and not on God's *law*. Be sure you understand the difference.

If there's a support group available for survivors of suicide loss within a reasonable distance, I highly recommend attending one. Your best supports will be others who've been there and understand the complications. Even in this scenario, though, you need to pick and choose wisely. Not every suicide grief survivor survives suicide grief. Many survive the experience but then stay forever stuck in fear, guilt, or anger. Many stay busy to avoid facing and working through their feelings. This is common but also dangerous, because grief will sit and wait but, in the end, *it will be heard.*

If you've attempted suicide or have already lost someone to suicide, *please don't wait* to get outside support. These experiences put your well-being at greater risk, and now isn't the time to carry this alone. If there's anything unhealed from your past, it will likely resurface now, and this can derail you within minutes. Navigating trauma is serious business, and although no one can really ease your suffering, they can *validate* it.

You need, now more than ever, to be seen and heard. Your grief needs to be honored because it represents the love you dared to share with the one you lost. It hurts terribly to let go, especially when you never got to say I love you, I'm sorry, or good-bye. Everyone will be touched by death at some point, but not everyone will be left with the haunting questions, disturbing images, or the heart-wrenching desperation that accompanies a suicide death. And thank God for that.

Just Say No

If you haven't established personal boundaries in this lifetime, now would be the perfect time to start. You'll only be able to handle so much during any given day, and there will probably be few people with whom you'll want to spend your precious time. This is not a bad thing, and it can work to your advantage.

Now is your time to decide who and what you want to allow into your personal space. I eliminated as many negative influences as possible, including the news (don't worry... you'll still hear about the big stuff), all other negative or violent media (including social media), and anything (and anyone) *which could potentially upset me.*

I guarded my heart as if my life depended on it. Negativity will drain your precious energy. Make it your mission to avoid it at any cost.

When you do use media for entertainment, try to find things that soothe or support you. Watch or listen to things that are lighthearted, gentle, or inspiring. Surround yourself with as much beauty, peace, and serenity as possible. This will initiate healing.

Decide with great care what to focus on, then focus only on that. Focus on one thing or one person at a time, one second, one minute, or one hour at a time, every day. Do as little as necessary to get by, so you can rest as often as possible. Grieving is hard work, and it is *exhausting.*

Learn to say no. If someone invites you out, and you don't want to go, *stay home.*

It's important to honor your feelings as well as your current physical state. You might be too exhausted for small talk right now, or you might just be uncomfortable in certain social situations. This is totally normal, and it's always okay to decline invitations when your body is screaming, "Oh, heck no!" Listen to it. It knows what you need.

Aside from your supports, there may be few people who reach out to you.

People tend to fear saying the wrong thing, so many won't even know how to approach the subject of your suicide loss. They might think saying nothing would be better than taking the risk of upsetting you more. (And who knows? They might be right.) It doesn't mean they don't care. They just might not know how to approach it.

Suicide loss is heavy, and not everyone can handle it. Keep this in mind but be relentless in your search for people who *can*. They are out there, and they're willing to sit with you without judgment. They know how to care for themselves, so you can feel free to show up as yourself, even when you're broken-hearted and bleeding. They won't get mad when you turn them down. They'll see all of you, and they'll love and respect you even more because you show up genuinely. You are a powerful survivor. Remember that.

My client, Melissa, became very frustrated when her friends kept pushing her into social situations. "They expect me to pick up where we left off and be the life of the party," she said, exhausted, "and I just don't have it in me to go *anywhere* right now." I assured her it was okay to listen to her body and tell them the truth. If she could be honest and set her own limits, her friends would probably understand. Well, they did, but she had to remind them several times before they finally caught on. Eventually, they left it up to her to reach out to them when she was ready, and Melissa was relieved she didn't have to put herself in those situations anymore, and she no longer goes out feeling manipulated or obligated. Now, she *chooses* to go when she feels up to it and wants to be around people.

Never underestimate the power of the word no. When life feels overwhelming and scary, it can be empowering to draw those lines in the sand.

Is Anybody Out There?

You might be at odds with God right now. Maybe you don't even know who God really is to you. If this is the case, nobody can blame you. Many of us have wrangled with faith or religion at some point. Personally, I'm not a fan of organized religion, but I believe in a Divine Source that loves and guides us all. If I didn't, I don't think I'd still be here.

I trust there's a plan and a purpose for everything because I see how, with each season, things inevitably come full circle. What seems nonsensical now will probably become clear in time. Life has a funny way of working itself out, and I don't believe that's coincidental. I've come to depend on this truth, and it's given me supernatural strength in times of darkness and confusion. I can't force you to believe in anything but, I know if I can somehow trust that a benevolent force (whatever name I choose to call it) sees me and has my best interest in mind, I'm never disappointed by the validation it offers along the way. Give it a try. You need the support, and the universe *wants* to support you. It's waiting, *without judgment*. Close your eyes, take a deep breath, and trust.

Your Tribe

Think of yourself as the chief of your tribe.

Your wisdom will guide you through this process. You are a true warrior by nature; both gentle and fierce. You know the next right step, even when you think you don't. As the leader of your life, you get to call most of the shots. Don't be afraid to harness your power, and don't be afraid to speak up for yourself.

The supports you assemble will share your workload and help keep you focused on the task at hand, which right now, is survival. They'll rally around you and jump in when needed. They *want* you to ask for help so they can lighten your load. So, ask. They will steer you away from negativity and tell you to trust yourself. They'll encourage you to slow down and breathe. They'll respect the journey. They'll respect you.

This road will be rocky but if you pour the foundation now, you'll be better equipped to handle whatever comes your way. You're not alone. You're *never* alone. The same force which guided me also guides you. You don't have to understand it, and you don't have to worry. Focus on the next thing and do *that*, every single day.

CHAPTER 5

Walk Gently into Your Process

"It doesn't matter how slowly you go as long as you
don't stop."
– Confucius

You didn't ask for this, and no, you didn't deserve it, either.

I will remind you again: Suicide is a *solitary* act. It had nothing to do with you *personally*. Suicide is more about *dis*connection – from others, and even more so, from the Self.

When I struggled with suicidality in my teens and twenties, I experienced extreme feelings of powerlessness, hopelessness, and separateness.

I believed I didn't belong. I had no real sense of who I was in relation to myself *or* in relation to others. I was, essentially, lost. This was a scary place because my mind played tricks on me (and I wholeheartedly believed its lies). I *believed* the world (and even my kids) would be better off without me. I *believed* I was a burden. I was trapped in a dangerous mindset, and *I had to find my way out of the darkness and back to myself.*

43

I want you to understand this as fact: You have no control over the thoughts or beliefs of another person. You have no control over their destiny. You are *only* in charge of yourself. In my opinion, this is more than enough, but our brains work tirelessly to make sense of devastation and the nonsensical. We create stories and blame ourselves or others because our unanswered questions are killing us. We'd rather blame ourselves than face our own powerlessness, but we aren't to blame. We're just desperate ... and searching.

Let's begin sifting through our own mess.

Dealing with your suicide grief will be more than enough to handle right now. Let's not complicate it by believing the lie that we can control anyone else. This process is about getting back to what matters to us: Our love and our lives. Happiness is still your birthright. Let's work through the hard stuff together so we can make space for the good that still lies ahead.

Honesty – The Best Policy

It's time to start trusting yourself.

You've been through the wringer, and there's no one in the world who knows what you need right now more than you do. (Even if you think you don't know, you always know.) Proceed gently and set an intention to grieve authentically. Your body will guide you.

Protect your heart, and avoid attention-hungry people, or anyone who makes you feel guilty or ashamed for taking care of yourself. If you don't, nobody else will.

The world will try to rush you, but this is *your* time and *your* experience. Respect your limits. Respect your feelings. Respect yourself.

I attended a picnic one weekend, within about three weeks of Elizabeth's death.

I was sitting alone (I didn't know the other guests) and I was content to watch the boats on the water without feeling obligated to make small talk with strangers I'd never see again. It was a nice afternoon and it felt good to be sitting outside in the sun. I was there, present, and very grateful not to have to cook that day. I'd already spent some time conversing with my friends, so this quiet time to myself was a soothing respite. I'd made the effort to attend the picnic and I thought it was going well, all things considered.

After about an hour or so my friend Steve came over to the table and told me I needed to "smile because I was bringing everyone down." (Nobody there knew me or anything about me. They were busy chatting amongst themselves and having a good time.) I looked at him incredulously, wondering why he was acting as if I'd been sitting there wailing and drawing attention to myself.

I looked at him matter-of-factly and said, "Steve, I just lost my sister. I might not be whooping it up at the moment, but I'm here and having a nice time. I'm not crying, and I haven't even brought it up. I'm okay, I'm just sitting here quietly enjoying the weather." He then informed me I needed to "get over" my loss and that I was "depressing." Stunned, I told him I wasn't willing to be fake to make him feel more comfortable. I felt strangely empowered in that moment. I don't see him anymore.

I'm aware his discomfort had nothing to do with me specifically.

He couldn't deal with his own feelings regarding suicide loss, so he needed me to pretend it never happened. Some people just can't deal, and that's okay. I need to express myself in a genuine way, so I'd rather avoid these kinds of people whenever possible.

> *"Feelings are just visitors, let them come and go."*
> – Mooji

I'm not sure when tears became so offensive or why grief and sadness are considered burdensome and "negative." Emotions are cleansing and merely energy in motion. They're not right or wrong. They simply *are*. I've noticed when I don't judge them, I don't tend to get stuck in them. If I can let them be what they need to be, without labeling them as negative or bad, they can move through me faster. If feelings weren't needed, we wouldn't have them. If people are offended by your grief, it's on them, not you. You have a right to take up space and to be authentic.

Not being honest about your emotions will only hijack your process.

Denying your feelings (whatever they may be) guarantees keeping you tied to them. The object here is to feel, admit, and release. Momentum is good and naming your emotions as they come up is an excellent practice. By naming them, you'll diffuse their intensity and *validate* yourself. This is both important and necessary. Now is not the time to pretend or hold back. This is *your life* we're talking about, and there's no time left to lose.

Stacy struggled with anger because, as a woman, she thought it was wrong to express it.

Instead, she fought it. She resisted, held it in, and refused to acknowledge it until, one day, someone cut her off on the highway. Infuriated, she laid on the horn and began screaming furiously at the driver in front of her. When we met later that day for our session, she admitted she'd been yelling at her kids over minor things she used to dismiss. We decided to try something new. Whenever she felt the familiar heat of anger, she would say, "I feel angry," out loud. This simple act of acknowledgment was enough to keep her from losing her cool in the moment. It also made her realize how often she was feeling it. Sometimes she'd have to repeat the statement a few times, but once she was heard and validated (by herself), she felt immediate relief.

Fighting is just too much work. It's so much easier to surrender. Don't get sucked into anyone else's rules, limitations, or timelines.

Always guard your heart and stay true to you. Honor yourself and your feelings. It's the fastest way to get to the other side. The only way to get out of pain is to actively *grieve*. This is much easier to do when surrounded by people who aren't spooked by your truth. Once you've given yourself permission to do this, go ahead and *mourn like a superhero.*

Your Way *Is* the Right Way

Don't worry about doing this wrong.

There is no right or wrong way to grieve, and no one can tell you how long your process will take. Each grief journey is different, and each has its own unique story. Rest assured your body already knows exactly what it needs to do to heal. If you listen closely, it will lead the way. It will tell you when to rage and when to cry. It will tell you when to rest and when to talk. It knows when it needs connection and when it would be better served in silence and solitude. It knows. Don't be afraid of your Inner Healer. It will help you.

Society has done a huge disservice by teaching us to minimize and stuff our pain. It's been proven that physical illness is a direct result of unresolved stress in the body.

I believe, for the most part, it's the same for mental illness. Still, our knee-jerk response to anything uncomfortable is to hide from it or numb it. Our pain doesn't need to be ignored or numbed any longer, though. It needs to be felt, acknowledged, and honored. Disease (like grief) is designed to slow us down and steer us back to ourselves, but that's not what we're taught, so many feel scared and alienated.

I'd like you to take a huge leap of faith today and look at grief as your friend, your confidant, and the All-Knowing Love Light which will eventually restore you to peace and happiness. I know it might seem counterintuitive, but I also know the more you resist reality, the longer you'll suffer.

Above all else, go easy.

Treat yourself and your body with tender loving kindness. It'll take all the strength you can muster to surf the unpredictable tides of suicide grief, and it will be exhausting. The more tuned in you are to yourself, the easier it will be to follow the ebb and flow of your personal process. Go mindfully and purposefully, but always, always go gently.

You Have a Right to Know

Sometimes people need details to find a greater sense of peace within their loss. Survivors differ in this area, and everyone must respect her own boundaries.

I needed to find and spend time in the place where Elizabeth died. I don't know why exactly – I just had to be there. It was part of my good-bye and my closure. I suppose it made it more real, because I had trouble wrapping my head around the actual suicide and the fact I'd never see her again. I took a trusted family member with me to find it, and then went back later alone, when I had more time to linger. It made me feel better somehow, just to be where she had been when she took her last breath.

Get your questions answered if you can and be sure to respect the limitations of other people, especially family members and friends. They must care for themselves too, and their process must be revered. This can be tough if you're grieving alone, and this is a good reason to have other solid supports in place.

You can always request copies of police or other applicable reports, if you feel you need them. Be sure to consider, though, if this information will ultimately help you or haunt you. Sometimes enough is enough. You must decide.

Permission to Grieve Exercise

I'd like to end this chapter by setting an intention.

On a plain sheet of paper, or in a designated notebook, I'd like you to write, sign, and date the following statement:

I, _____, grant myself permission to wholeheartedly grieve, in my own way and for as long as it takes, to honor my life and the life of my beloved, _____ _____, to receive the highest healing possible. And so it is.

_____

Sign and Date

The Survivor's Bill of Rights:

- You have a right to grieve in your own way and in your own time
- You have a right to *all* your feelings
- You have a right to be seen, heard, and acknowledged
- You have a right to know the details surrounding your loved one's death

- You have a right to decline invitations and/or modify plans
- You have a right to say no
- You have a right to ask for help
- You have a right to be angry at God
- You have a right to let go of guilt
- You have a right to a full recovery and a happy life

CHAPTER 6

Align with Your Inner Healer

*"Sometimes when one person is missing, the whole
world feels depopulated."*
– Lamartine

Now that you have your supports in place, and you've given yourself permission to grieve in a way that honors you, you're ready to create your sacred healing space. This will be a cocoon of sorts and the place you'll likely spend most of your downtime in the coming weeks and months.

Please be sure it's as quiet and comfortable as possible. Anything you can do to make it feel warmer or more inviting will be a huge bonus. Think of this room as the conduit that connects you to your Inner Healer.

Be sure to set boundaries around who may enter the room and when.

You need to feel safe here. This is *your* space and can be whatever you need it to be right now. Just be sure you can completely relax, unwind, and nap there. You need at least one physical space where you can show up, *exactly as you are in any given moment,* without having to explain yourself to anyone or pretend to be okay.

A bedroom, den, office space, or even a rec room will work, if it isn't a common room and you're certain to have some actual privacy. I realize this can be difficult if you live with small children or if you're married and this space happens to be your bedroom. Do the best you can with what you have. The main goal is to find safety and relief from the demands and expectations of the world. You'll need as much down time as you can get, so don't allow anyone to make you feel guilty about this. Rest is vital to your health and well-being.

Grieving and mourning are hard work and require large chunks of time for quiet solitude, restoration, and integration. Please don't underestimate the importance of this step. This room will quickly become (if it hasn't already) your room of choice, and your space to get *real* to completely heal.

If others live in the house, explain that you'll need as much quiet time as possible now to work through your loss. Always be honest and let them know ahead of time if you're feeling particularly fried or exhausted that day. Since people are wrapped up in their own stuff, you might want to give them a heads-up about where you're at so they'll be more likely to understand and respect your boundaries. If you leave them guessing they might unconsciously act carelessly, worry about you, or think you're angry with *them*. Never assume people know what's going on with you. They aren't mind-readers, no matter how much we wish they were.

Staying real about your feelings is a good boundary-keeping practice, because it will remind you to avoid worrying about other people's feelings. Stay in your own business. Be open, real, and responsible for yourself. It'll be much better for you and everyone else.

Own Your Experience

You have a right and a responsibility to care for yourself now.

Nobody else in the world knows what you need like you do. For a long time, I believed others would know what I needed and offer it without my having to ask. Not only was this unfair, it was also unreasonable. I didn't tell them what I needed, so how in the world could they possibly

know? Through osmosis? Maybe. I remember thinking, "It's common sense! Why doesn't he/she...?" Yet, I never opened my mouth. Consequently, I often didn't get what I needed and often felt resentful.

Eventually, I learned we all have different experiences and varied ways of dealing with things, so my needs wouldn't automatically jive with someone else's and vice versa. I decided to stop wishing and waiting for someone to come to my rescue, and I rescued myself. I simply asked for what I needed.

Take charge of your experience, because it's *all yours*.

Don't be afraid to ask for what you need and if you don't get it, ask again or ask someone else. There are people out there who are ready to support you. As I mentioned earlier, they don't always end up being the people you started with, and they also might not be who you expected. Sometimes you need to search high and low for people who "get" you, but trust me when I tell you, they exist and they're waiting for you. The more you connect to yourself, the more easily you'll attract what you need.

Your Inner Connection

No one else's journey will be exactly like yours.

While there may be similarities, all will have different needs and different limitations. There are simply too many variables to compare and, if you've had more than one loss, your process might take longer than someone else's. That's okay. This isn't a race. Go slow and accept where you are right now. You won't stay here forever if you can be okay with what lives within you. Always follow your body.

"What is lovely never dies, but passes into another loveliness, star dust or sea foam, flower or winged air."
– Thomas Bailey Aldrich

Ask your Inner Healer to meet you in your sacred space each morning.

You can ask out loud or in your mind. Ask it to guide you throughout your day and to help you to become aware of what needs attention in the present moment. Sit quietly, focus inward, and pay attention to what happens in your body and your mind. Become aware of feelings that surface, images or thoughts that arise, and any physical pain or tension you experience. These cues will become your guides. Follow them, and you'll stay on track.

If you feel like crying, cry. Your Inner Healer is nudging you.

If you're tired, take a nap or rest if you can. Your Inner Healer is trying to slow you down. If you don't feel like being around people, go to your sacred space for some solitude and quiet. Your Inner Healer knows when you need to protect your energy. If you feel like screaming or raging, yell into a pillow or go someplace safe where you can let it all out. Your Inner Healer knows you need to release intense feelings to avoid displacing emotions onto others and falling into major depression.

What you don't deal with in the moment, you'll only have to deal with later.

If, for any reason, you're unable to deal with it in the moment, don't worry. Another chance will present itself. Sometimes intense emotions will come at inopportune times. Do the best you can. If you don't intentionally inhibit the process, you won't do it wrong. Go slowly, but don't stop. Yes, you can take breaks, but try not to run away.

At this point, you may or may not be experiencing a full myriad of emotions, but I'm certain you're probably feeling *something*. Whatever it is, try not to be afraid of it. Name it (if you can) and practice "being" with it without judgment. Words, thoughts, or images might come up with the feelings.

Pay attention to these and write them down in a note-book whenever possible. These messages might come in handy later, once you've had some time to recover and reflect.

You can pretty much expect to feel just about anything right now including panic, terror, and despair. Feelings of powerlessness are also very common in suicide loss survivors, and you may also be experiencing intense anger and rage. If you're still in shock you might be stunned or feeling nothing. *Assume all feelings are normal* and go with whatever is. The trick is to hold back as little as possible and release the emotions as soon as possible.

Please understand that I'm talking about releasing emotions safely and productively. It's never okay to unload or unleash anger or rage onto others. In Chapter 8, I'll show you how to deal with the more intense emotions without harming yourself or anyone else. For now, I want you to get a firm handle on the messages your body is sending and honor them to the best of your ability.

Embrace Possibility

I'm going to ask you once more to open yourself up to the idea that a higher being, who loves you dearly and sees you in this time of desperation, will undoubtedly create something beautiful out of this tragedy. Rest assured your suffering is witnessed and your tears are counted. You *and* your pain matter because it all boils down to love. It's the only reason we're here, and you dared to love so deeply. If you hadn't, you wouldn't be in this agony. You did what you came here to do and you did it well. You weren't really left behind. Death is only an illusion. Believe you're loved, supported, and already have everything you need within and around you to get through this. It's time to *honor you*. You're ready. Let's do this ... together.

CHAPTER 7

Know and Speak Your Truth

"Let my inner weeping arise and blossom."
– Rainer Maria Rilke

If you only remember one thing from this book, let it be this:

Silence can be deadly. The best thing you can do for yourself and the people around you now is to speak as openly and honestly as possible about the way you're feeling. I realize you won't always feel like talking and that's okay, but when you do, make a deliberate effort to make it count. Rest assured your Inner Healer will lead the way by providing a sense of urgency when talking will be of most benefit to you. Please honor this urgency, because relief will inevitably follow, even if it takes some time.

The pain will be intense at first, and the more you can follow the inner urges of your aching heart, the more your body will learn to trust you as its navigator. Remember, you are in charge, because only you know what's true and what works best for you. Always, always follow your gut. It never lies.

Talk Until You're Blue in the Face

Initially, it's good practice to talk about the suicide death itself. Often.

Repeating the story out loud and saying the word *suicide* will help the experience become more real so you can begin to believe it. I know you might not want to believe it, but telling and retelling your story will help you come to terms with the tragic loss of your loved one. Although denial is a normal part of the grieving process, you can't fully make peace with something you refuse to accept. This is a slow and steady process, so give yourself a break. Do the best you can to keep the lines of communication open.

Tell your story to your trusted supports as often as needed, and don't hold *any* feelings back. Take care to honor *whatever* comes up without judgment, as this will help you avoid the pitfalls of guilt (which are also normal but can quickly send you into deep depression if you're not paying close attention). Your thoughts and feelings, whatever they may be, need to be heard and acknowledged with compassion.

People might inadvertently try to interrupt you, offer platitudes, or even be surprised by your words or your honesty. Don't let these reactions throw you or shut you down. Sometimes people feel desperate to rescue or just aren't sure what to say. This usually has more to do with their issues than yours. Give them the benefit of the doubt, thank them, and tell them you only need to be witnessed and heard. Nothing more. They will be relieved, and you won't have to take it personally.

Many will offer sympathy rather than empathy and this can be hard to swallow. Those who haven't been through suicide loss often have a difficult time wrapping their heads around it. The words "I'm so sorry for your loss" sound a lot different than "What a shame," but either one of these statements can make you feel as though you're being brushed off or patted on the head. I found statements like that latter to be callous and thoughtless and would've gladly settled for silence instead, but I had to keep in mind they were doing the best they could with the resources *they* had.

You'll probably be sensitive to the words of others now, but if your safe people are lined up and know how you need them to respond to you, they'll be able to do so in more favorable ways. It's your job to tell them what you need from them. Be as open as possible, and you'll get much better results. Remember, silence serves no one: not you and certainly not anyone else.

Just Say It

Make sure you have the freedom to speak freely with at least one person.

When I say freely, I mean you can say anything without fear of freaking another person out or turning them away. This does not mean you won't be held accountable for your words, it simply means the other person promises to hold you in the highest regard no matter what you tell them.

There might be times you're feeling desperate to end your own pain. It's of utmost importance to express those feelings.

This is completely normal after suicide loss, and you need to be free enough to honor the desperate feelings too. However, you also need to have a plan in place in case you need additional support to get through a particularly rocky time. Again, this is normal, and if someone is genuinely worried about your mental or physical state, you would be wise to come up with a safety plan. Be sure to keep your support numbers accessible so you can find them easily if need be. Include both the National Suicide Prevention Lifeline (800-273-8255) and the Crisis Text Line (text "hello" to 741741) in case you'd like an additional option.

Often, just speaking about and admitting to our desperate thoughts and intense feelings will release their emotional charge, but please be sure to choose your listeners carefully, and *never unload on children*. Sometimes we just need a break from regular responsibilities because of overwhelm and exhaustion. It's okay to ask for help, and people are probably waiting for a chance to be of service to you. Churches are a great resource during times like these, especially if cooking, cleaning, or childcare is needed. If you need to create a safety plan immediately, please visit My Safety Plan located in Chapter 9.

Now is not the time to hold back the truth, no matter what it may be.

Believe me when I tell you, someone will be able to handle it. I remember sitting in my pastor's office, shortly after my sister died. I was angry, hurt, and felt completely powerless. She sensed my despair. I said, "I just feel like…"

I couldn't finish the sentence. I was afraid she'd call 911 and have me involuntarily committed. "Just say it," she said, "It needs to come out." I said the forbidden words, "I just want to go too! I want to be with her!" The world didn't end, she didn't call 911, and she didn't have me committed. She *was* concerned and made me promise that I'd do whatever necessary to keep myself safe and follow up with my counselor, which I did.

Ironically (or not), just saying those desperate words released me from their spell. This stuck with me, and I've made sure to accept and release these thoughts since, the moment I have them. They're only thoughts. I'm allowed to both have and express them.

I don't have to act on them, though, and neither do you.

Grieve Ugly

I am not a believer in holding back feelings although I did, in many areas of my life, for decades. Mostly, I feared ridicule, resentment, and retribution.

Who did I think I was, anyway? Wasn't it better to keep quiet and keep the peace?

No! Not when your life is at stake. After my suicide loss, all bets were off, and I had to decide if I was going to put up and shut up or get real and get to work. I opted for the latter and let it all hang out. I talked until I was blue in the face. No regrets. I'm here and finally happy! Go figure.

Hold back nothing.

I believe it's important to be honest with yourself first before you can be honest with others. It's usually easy to remember happy memories with our loved ones, but what do we do with the not-so-happy ones?

Sometimes people think it's blasphemous to speak "unkindly" of the deceased, and I encourage you to embrace whatever reality you know to be true. Nobody's perfect, and you're not required to *only* remember the "good times." We're human and we all have our shortcomings and quirks. In fact, you might find a lot of healing when speaking about the truths that were less than savory. It's all fair game and all part of the process.

Experience whatever is revealed to you with empathy and grace.

There may be a smaller version of you inside who needs some love and reassurance. Suicide survivors are unexpectedly dropped into a wilderness of fear and uncertainty. This fear can make us raw and vulnerable when exposed to the outside world. It's okay to take care of this inner child right now and keep her safe for a while. Ask her what she needs and what she has to say. Hold her and rock her. Sing her to sleep. This is when it starts to get real. It will probably feel scary and it might even get ugly. Follow it anyway. The young versions of ourselves know the way better than we do. They know what they need, so listen to their words and follow their lead. Let them grieve in their own unique way.

I'd like you to embrace your reality whenever you can, even when it doesn't feel good. This can be difficult, and you don't have to like it. Just *be* with whatever *is*. Trust it has a purpose. If it's rage, sadness, or blame, get ugly when you talk (or yell) about it. Let the words out and make them *big*. Intentionally *become* the feeling, and let the words flow until you feel relief. The more you can learn to do this, to really lean in, own, and express your truth, the less energy you'll have to spend resisting and revisiting those dark places later. Silence and resistance are the main causes of struggle and suffering. Most people don't understand this, but if you can get a firm grasp on this truth you'll be way ahead of the game, and this grief experience will become more tolerable.

The Whys

Everybody wonders *why*. Why did this happen?

Why didn't I see this coming? Why couldn't I help him/her? Why do I have to go through this? Why did he/she leave me like this? While this is normal, I recommend you don't stay here too long. These are questions you might never get answered, and to entertain them day and night will not only drain you, they will disempower you. I recommend getting any actual answers you can, but questions like "why me" can keep you stuck in victimhood, especially if not confronted.

It's important to release these why questions to your loved one, because they're fair questions. Ask them. Scream them at the top of your lungs if you need to. I did. I didn't think we deserved to be left that way and I was enraged. I let everyone have it. (I was alone in the house at the time.) I screamed at my sisters, my parents, and God. I screamed until I broke down sobbing on my living room floor. I was sure my chest would explode from the pressure, and that the pain I felt would kill me.

But I survived. Again. Was this my punishment for trying to end my own life? No. I don't think so, but it was important for me to ask my why questions before I could finally let them go.

The actions of our loved ones belong to *them*.

The actions we take from this point on are *our* responsibility. Why does anything bad happen to anyone? Because it does. Bad things happen to good people every day. Everyone gets a turn in this spotlight (maybe multiple turns) and it doesn't mean we're cursed or that this misery will be our destiny.

We decide how we want to live and experience our lives from this moment forward. It's our choice. Life wasn't punishing me, and I didn't have this coming. It happened. Now, I can decide it happened *to* me and remain a victim, or I can decide to take charge of myself, my feelings, and my experience and make change happen *through* me. I'd much rather be an agent for change. It's far more empowering.

Be intentional. Know your truth and don't be afraid to speak it.

This experience is sacred and yours alone. You owe it to yourself and your loved one to show up, just as you are, and say it like it is. Maybe nobody else will, and that's not your problem. Your job is to be mindful of only you. How lucky you are to be one of the few!

Feel, Realize, and Release Exercise

This is an exercise I recommend doing each morning after you wake up and each evening before you go to sleep. Be sure the room is completely quiet, and you won't be interrupted by pets, children, or spouses. Give yourself about a half hour to complete this in the morning and about 15 minutes in the evening.

Sit straight up or lay flat on your back. Close your eyes and focus on your breath.

Place one hand on your heart and one on your belly. Ask your Inner Healer to offer you guidance. Once you've settled in, scan your body beginning at the top of your head down to the tips of your toes. Make a mental note of any tightness or tension along the way, releasing it as needed. Once you're completely relaxed, pay attention to any discomfort, feelings, or thoughts that arise. If your mind begins to wander, return your focus to the breath until you settle in again. You may hear a message or see images. These are signs. Follow your body and listen closely. If you have a specific question, ask your Inner Healer. If not, you can simply ask what you need to focus on that day. When you feel you have an answer, open your eyes and get your journal or notebook.

Write your intention (aim or focus) for the day (for example: I am healing and whole, or I will speak up when I'm angry, or I will accept my sadness without judgment, etc.).

Write down the thoughts, feelings, stories, or images you experienced during your meditation, without censoring them. Use strong language and curse words if you need to and get it all out onto the paper until you feel empty. There's no wrong way to do this exercise. If writing is difficult for you, speak your thoughts and feelings into your phone and record them that way instead.

Revisit your journal in the evening and add anything that came up throughout the day. Leave nothing out. This is your chance to say it all, however you need to. It isn't necessary to write in narrative form. If you want to list feelings and random, fragmented thoughts, that's fine too. Just get it all out. Before you go to sleep, thank your Inner Healer for showing up and leading the way.

This exercise will get you in touch with your body and your feelings and will also help create space for deep healing. Please be encouraged because this *will* get easier.

CHAPTER 8

Emotions Are Necessary

"There may be days I curl up in a blanket with my coffee
and just cry. Cry because the pain of letting go is almost
as painful as the initial loss."
– S.S. Jubilee

The Emotional Rollercoaster

There's no doubt that you'll experience every possible human emotion on this journey. Some feelings will be easier than others to manage, and all seem to have their place and purpose, even the explosive ones. Shock, disbelief, and numbing help you to survive the initial impact of the news. This is your body's way of protecting you until your brain has time to catch up to the reality of your loss. Each experience is different, and each person comes to terms with suicide loss in their own way. You might find yourself in and out of this state for quite a while, especially if you didn't see your loved one on a regular basis.

Once the shock wears off, anger and despair can take over, along with intense fear and helplessness. I can't stress enough that every feeling has its place, and none need to be avoided. The trick will be to get through each one as it presents itself, and rest as much as possible until the next wave hits. The waves will hit at random times, so you won't always be able to prepare yourself. This is one of the reasons time in solitude is so important. The body and mind need rest to keep up with the relentless demands of grieving. Just about any feeling is possible now, so I'm going to try to address one basic emotion at a time and expand from there.

Anger

Anger can mask as irritability, hostility, upset, resentment, agitation, short temperedness, reactivity, frustration, hatefulness, bitterness, rebelliousness, impatience, sarcasm, disrespect, spitefulness, and even jealousy. You might wonder how some of these words could apply, but you need to be aware that people don't always feel safe with their anger, so it often comes out in other, "safer" ways.

You might believe you're okay with your anger, or at least have it in check, until you realize you've been overreacting to small annoyances you once brushed off. Or perhaps you find yourself resenting people who have mothers because yours is now gone. Again, these feelings are normal when anger builds to the point of overflow, so you simply need to be mindful and real with yourself. If you're reacting to things that didn't used to bother you, it might be good to face your anger head-on and do a Feel, Realize, and Release Exercise. Don't be afraid to call it what it is. The truth will always set you free.

Also keep in mind that underneath anger is usually a lot of hurt.

Anger acts as a protective shield, but when it's stripped away, we're often left aching, tormented, crushed, and humiliated. Deal with the anger, but always be sure to address the pain that lies beneath it. You'll most likely find a young child who needs your time and attention. Please be sure to validate her. She's been shattered too.

About six months into my grief I started experiencing stomach pains, and I thought I might be getting an ulcer. At this point, I wasn't verbally expressing the depth of my frustration, confusion, or anger regarding the state of a significant relationship, so these feelings turned into major gastric upset. The H-Pylori test came back negative, but my blood work indicated problems with my pancreas. After further testing, we found out my gallbladder was only functioning at 17% and it needed to be removed. They thought I had stones, but there was an anomaly in one of the ducts, so it and the gall bladder had to go.

I was told later gallbladder problems were associated with unexpressed anger, according to Chinese medicine. This made sense to me because of the symptoms I was experiencing: pain, burning, irritation, digestive problems … it wasn't rocket science, and the body never lies. People who hold onto anger also tend to have chronic neck, shoulder, and arm pain. My shoulder was killing me, and not coincidentally.

I decided from then on to become more deliberate about expressing my anger, especially physically. The following are some of the exercises I've used to release the explosive feelings of rage and blame. Of course, I recommend verbal expression too, whenever possible and as soon as possible to keep the energy moving through you. Remember: Honesty is always the best policy.

Twisting Towels

Take a bath towel and fold it in half to shorten it.

Roll it up as you would a yoga mat. With one hand on either end, twist it until you can't twist anymore. The harder you twist it, the greater release you'll get. Really feel your anger within, and make whatever sounds you need to, as you're twisting. Gnashing your teeth, grunting, or saying whatever words you need to say will make this exercise more powerful and effective. Don't hold back and keep going until you feel enough of a release to stop or you tire yourself out. Rest and repeat if necessary.

Batter Up!

Disclaimer: This exercise can work with a real bat or a toy bat, but please be careful how and where you use it, so you don't break anything (including yourself). You can also use gloves to help you get a better grip on the bat if you find it helpful, and if you have back problems you might want to skip this exercise or modify the process.

Gather a pile of large cushions or pillows and place them on the floor in an open area. (Couch and large floor pillows work best for this exercise.) Kneel on the floor in front of the pillows. Grip the bat firmly *with both hands,* one fist on top of the other (as if you were up to bat at a game). Raise the bat over your head and hit the pillows repeatedly as hard as you can. Again, it helps to verbally express your anger at the same time, so yell, scream, grunt, curse, or do whatever your body needs to release. Rest and repeat if necessary.

Mosaic Project

It's been my experience while dealing with anger and other explosive emotions, that the sound of breaking glass can feel strangely satisfying. If you happen to have some old dishes lying around, or you can grab some for next to nothing at a flea market or thrift store, this exercise can be cathartic.

Take a small box of old dishes out to the garage (preferably by yourself so nobody gets hurt). Put on a pair of safety glasses and throw the dishes directly and deliberately, one at a time, into an empty trash can. Listen to them shatter. If you feel led to yell and holler, go for it – you just might want to give your neighbors a heads-up that everyone and everything is okay before you start. If you don't want to explain yourself, tell them you're helping a friend with a mosaic project. This exercise, when done safely, can be very gratifying (and if you do mosaic, you can repurpose the glass)!

Dragon Breathing Exercise

This exercise was introduced to me as fire breathing, and it's very effective if you can't or don't want to practice the primal scream. Personally, screaming hurts my throat and makes me hoarse for days, so I found this exercise to be a great alternative.

Imagine yourself as a giant dragon. Close your eyes, put your hand on your belly, and slowly breathe in, making your belly expand as it fills up with air. Release the breath slowly and deliberately, while making a hissing sound through your teeth (as a cat would). Imagine this breath is fire as you push the air out of your dragon's mouth. This fire will protect and purify you. It can be any color you like, and it can burn anything in your way. Once the exhale is complete, repeat as needed. Own and feel your power. You can do this repeatedly. It also helps to imagine breathing in purity and breathing out toxicity. Go with whatever works for you, just remember to hiss.

Fear

Fear is a big obstacle for suicide loss survivors and it also masquerades as anxiety, worry, suspicion, panic, apprehension, dread, rigidity, intolerance, avoidance, paranoia, defensiveness, and sometimes even paralysis. C.S. Lewis said, "I never knew grief felt so much like fear." This quote never felt truer to me than after suicide loss. Death, especially a suicide death, reminds us of our fragility, both physically and emotionally. This can be unnerving, especially if the person you lost always seemed to have it together (or at one time had it together). We're reminded of our own mortality and/or our own tendencies toward depression and hopelessness. This terrified me and, for months, I was unable to sleep at all without medication. Anxiety and panic were huge energy drains for me, and nothing depleted me faster.

Some of the physical manifestations of anxiety may include: shortness of breath, heart palpitations (or pounding), shakiness or trembling, excessive sweating, dizziness or light-headedness, nausea, vomiting, difficulty swallowing, hot and cold flashes, and choking sensations.

Some survivors live with the memories of discovering their loved one or having to identify their body. I'm eternally grateful this wasn't part of my journey. If this applies to you, please do whatever you need to do to soothe and comfort yourself and call on professionals for extra support if need be, at least for a while.

Once again, I will remind you to express any fears you have regarding your suicide loss or your current reality. You might, at times, feel as though you're coming unglued. This, believe it or not, is also normal. Give your nervous system time to settle down and learn to relax again. This is going to take some time, so try to be patient with yourself as you heal.

Take tiny steps into the world whenever you feel strong enough to do so, but when you've had enough, go back to your safe healing space to rest and regroup. You'll learn your limits early on, because being visible during this tender time is extremely exhausting. Your body will need a lot of rest now. Respect it and listen to it. Doing so will keep you from becoming physically and emotionally ill.

In times of intense anxiety, I found the Dragon Breathing Exercise previously mentioned to be of great help. You might need some additional help to manage your fearful thoughts and panic for a while, and this is very common for suicide loss survivors. I highly recommend doing guided relaxation or meditations every day, at least twice a day (morning and evening). There are lots of meditations available for free on YouTube, and you can find them on Spotify and Pandora as well. Carving out time for guided relaxation or meditation will be one of the best things you can do to heal your body, your mind, and your anxiety.

You've been traumatized, and it's natural to feel shaky. If your anxiety becomes straight up insomnia and you can't get any restful sleep (and you might not for a while), cut back on caffeine or cut it out altogether, and switch to herbal tea. If panic, anxiety, and insomnia persist, *please don't hesitate to visit your medical or homeopathic doctor.* They're trained to help the grieving.

The main goal is to try to live in the present moment as much as possible.

Traumatic memories drag us backward, and we need to remember to bring ourselves back into the here and now, so our bodies can learn we are safe and not stuck in the past. This too, is a practice and will become easier in time.

Grounding Techniques

Name your feelings out loud as you're experiencing them. If you're anxious say, "I feel anxious," then find where you feel it in your body. This will help you reconnect within and become more mindful at the same time. Naming the feelings also helps them let go of *you*. The more you resist or try to ignore them, the louder they'll become to get your attention. They only want to be heard, so go ahead and give them some satisfaction. Believe me, it'll make you feel a lot better.

Here are few other easy things you can do to ground yourself when you become anxious:

- Trace your hand
- Focus on only your breath for five minutes
- Go out in nature and name what you see
- Take off your shoes and walk in the grass
- Stretch
- Hold an ice cube
- Name five things you can see in your room
- Name two things you can hear
- Call a friend

Sadness

Sadness may also be experienced as anguish, loneliness, dismay, remorse, fragility, disconnectedness, discontentedness, and devastation. Sadness is probably one of the more "acceptable" feelings on the grief spectrum, and maybe one of the easier ones to release if you're a woman and/or you tend to cry easily. Tears are cleansing and detoxifying. If you feel the urge to cry, don't hold them back. They will strengthen you.

Sobbing is especially productive and powerful, because it shakes loose those deep feelings of remorse and devastation, so they can make their way up and out.

If you tend to hold back or hold in, you'll be more prone to depression, moodiness, and even shame. Think of your tears as powerful healers. Invite them to visit often. You'll almost always feel better after a good, hard cry, and it's one of the faster ways to relief.

The physical manifestations of your sadness and grief might also include: chest pain, difficulty breathing, swelling in your body, headaches, muscle aches, forgetfulness, loss of appetite, gain in appetite, and even a feeling that you, yourself, might be dying. No, you are *not* crazy. A part of you *has* died, the old you, and it's going to hurt for a while until you can figure out who the new you will be.

Be gentle with yourself. This is a time of deep sorrow, and you didn't get to say good-bye.

Sadness just comes with the territory. Some might believe you need to "snap out of it," and in good time, you will. Until then, let the tears flood your neighborhood. There's nothing more healing, and they're nobody's business but yours.

About Confusion and Helplessness

Confusion and helplessness were two of the more difficult emotions for me, and for a while, I feared I might be losing my mind. I was disoriented, easily confused, forgetful, indecisive, and generally perplexed. There were few people I trusted, and everything I thought I knew had come undone. My world seemed to be spinning out of control and I was helpless to fix or stop it. I was at my wit's end, exhausted from living and exhausted from grieving.

I'd done my best to care for myself and my family, but I had nothing left to give. I was so depleted I couldn't eat, sleep, or do anything other than the minimum required to survive. I was breaking down, and I had to ask for more help. I didn't have the energy to drive myself an hour to therapy twice a week, so we started doing more sessions over the phone. My kids picked up the slack at home, so I could lay down and rest after work. I stopped resisting my fatigue and eventually (if not somewhat begrudgingly) accepted my new limits. I was no longer Wonder Woman. Those days, apparently, were over.

If you can relate in any way to this, you can see you're not alone.

There was more than one time I thought I might end up hospitalized and, looking back, I think it was due to overwhelm and exhaustion. When I finally asked for help and accepted my own limitations, that's when the deep healing really began. There's power in surrender. You finally let go of expectations and accept what you can do and what you can't. There are no awards for doing this alone, and believe me when I tell you, we are not meant to do this alone. I urge you to ask for help and accept it with grace. It'll be the most empowering thing you ever do for yourself. You deserve some relief. Go ahead and ask for some.

Guilt: The Other Four-Letter Word

Yes, guilt is probably the number one nemesis of suicide loss survivors, and one of the most difficult with which to come to terms. Genuine healing cannot occur if you're chained to the belief that the suicide death was somehow your fault. This belief is simply not true but, as humans, we'd rather blame ourselves than deal with the fact that we have no control over the beliefs and decisions of another person. Again, our brains are desperately trying to build a story around what is unknown.

I urge you to write this down and post it all over your house: *I am not to blame. It wasn't my fault.*

Let yourself off the hook. Holding onto guilt won't bring them back, but it will help you dig your own grave, if only metaphorically. You deserve so much better than this. As a survivor of traumatic loss, you deserve a full recovery and a sublimely happy existence. Take back what's rightly yours and *decide* to leave guilt behind. As always, talk about these feelings with a trusted source who can offer an objective perspective, but understand guilt for what is really is: a quick and convenient answer to tremendously complex and unanswerable questions.

The Grief Purge Exercise

I'd like to offer you one more exercise you can use when feeling general overwhelm.

This is a quick writing exercise and will require one side of a blank sheet of paper. Begin the sentence "I feel ..." and write down every word that pops into your mind.

Once your list is complete, read each feeling out loud to yourself. When you're finished, say, "Thank you for showing up. I see you, I hear you, I honor you." Then tear it up or put it through the shredder. Nicely done! You've just completed The Grief Purge.

I hope I've convinced you that it's imperative to acknowledge and feel to heal.

There's just no easy way around it. You'll likely stay out of trouble if you give yourself the time to be still and listen, every day. Your Inner Healer wants to help you. Follow your body's lead and keep speaking your truth. Release physically as you're prompted and be sure to ask for help when you need it. Keep telling your stories and release yourself from guilt. I promise you're not going crazy, and you can survive this experience. Take it one feeling at a time, one hour at a time. You can handle almost anything for one hour. You've got this, and I've got you.

CHAPTER 9

Nurture Your Needs

Though gone,
you are here.
I feel it...
my soul.
Each step
teaching and guiding
back to books,
pens... and colors.
They waited patiently...
my friends.
Hello again.

Now that you're learning to accept and manage your feelings, you'll also need to figure out how to best tend to your needs and your precious energy. You're taking on giants right now, and this is *not* the time to take on large projects or make any major decisions. Please give yourself a break and adequate time to heal before taking on extra stuff. Believe me, it will wait. You've been through so much, and if there was ever a time to consider radical self-love practices, the time is *now*. Let's focus on finding ways to soothe and restore your body, mind, and soul. Like previous chapters, this one will offer many different suggestions. I encourage you to try them all and add whatever needed so you can decide what activities work best for you. You might find what works on one day won't on another. As always, let your Inner Healer lead the way.

There's no right or wrong here. The idea is to rest, relax, and restore yourself as never before. You *deserve* to be nurtured. After all, if you won't care for yourself, who else will? I can't think of a better time than now for bodacious self-love, so let's begin.

Naps

Since you're probably not sleeping very well at night, feel free to nap, whenever possible, during the day. These naps don't need to be long to be effective. Many people find 10-20-minute naps very refreshing. Personally, I almost never nap less than an hour or two, and I napped *a lot* during the first year of my loss. It was the only sound sleep I really got, and it helped me greatly to have this regular quiet time scheduled into my day: a chunk of time when nobody needed me for anything.

Scheduling time for peace and solitude will provide your mind and body the space and freedom you need to unwind, reflect, and integrate. Make this practice sacred and do whatever it will take to get at least one hour of uninterrupted time for yourself each day. If you can hire a sitter, do it. Solicit as much help as possible to give yourself the gift of solitude. You'll look forward to this time and it really will help you heal.

Finding Beauty

Spend time in nature whenever you can. Connecting to your surroundings will make you feel less alone. Really get your senses involved and make it your mission to find something beautiful every day. Walk around and take pictures of what you see. When something catches your eye, stop. Study it. Notice the natural order of nature. There's no agenda. No rush. Just exquisite artistry. Everything has its place. Everything belongs.

Notice what you see, smell, and hear. Take time to touch things. Take off your shoes and walk barefoot in the grass. Feel the earth under your feet. Realize you are part of everything that is. Realize you are still alive and you still belong.

Go wherever you feel inspired. I love the water, so I visit the beach in my hometown whenever possible. Both of my sisters took me there as a kid, so they tend to show up during these visits as rainbows, sparrows, and even written messages. On one trip, I sat down with my coffee on the only flat, comfortable rock I could find. I sat, mesmerized by the water while happily reminiscing over childhood memories with a friend, and when my gaze eventually wandered down and to the right of my feet, I saw the words "I love you" etched into the rock in front of me with an arrow above it pointing directly at my shoes. (This one really shook me up, and it took me the rest of the day to regain my composure.) I've been back there since but never found that message again.

During another trip to the lake, I climbed those same rocks with my kids. I sat with my son next to the water and I told him how much my sisters loved it there too. I told him about the message they left me and how it was one of our favorite places to surf waves, write in the sand, and skip stones. I wasn't aware that my daughter's friend was taking pictures of us at the time. When she later showed them to me, she pointed out a strange halo of light surrounding both of us. Apparently, we weren't alone that day either.

Connecting to nature helps you to connect to yourself.

I can't think of a better place to find peace and order when your world feels completely out of control. Nature is the reminder we are part of something much bigger than ourselves, and this truth can bring us back to a sense of deep peace and normalcy.

The Walking Meditation

Charlene often walked with her dog. As part of her meditation practice, we included an exercise to help her connect to nature and ease her anxiety.

As they took their daily stroll, Charlene would notice something and name it by using only a one-word description: bird, flower, tree. As she spoke the word, she'd focus intently on it, looking at it as if for the very first time. This calmed her nervous system and brought her so much unexpected joy that she began taking more frequent walks just to look for something new. Nature can be incredibly healing, especially when combined with this simple meditative practice.

Positive Plugins

Once again, I want to remind you to avoid negativity. This is the last thing your delicate nervous system needs right now. Nothing will drain your precious energy faster than exposure to negative Nellies (or any other negative sources, including the news and other fear-based or violent media). The world will keep spinning on its axis, and you'll still find out what's happening out there, but there is no need to place yourself on the front lines when you're already fragile. You'll be better served by filling your weary mind with sounds, images, and messages which will feed and uplift you. Choose wisely. Listen to inspirational podcasts and beautiful music. Watch movies that make you happy and, dare I say, make you laugh. (Yes! It's still okay to laugh.)

Read books that fill your mind with magnificent visions and endless possibilities. Feed your soul. Feed your mind. Forget about the world for a while. Those problems will take more than a season to resolve anyway. You have enough to handle now. Give yourself permission to turn away and nourish yourself. You deserve to feel hopeful again.

Creative Expression

If you're feeling the need to express yourself in non-verbal ways, now would be a great time to tap into some creative, artistic expression. Let's face it, talking becomes exhausting after a while and sometimes narratives don't do our feelings justice. If this is the case for you, choose an activity that will free you from speaking altogether. Activities like dancing, creating art, or playing music can provide amazing relief for grieving people. Singing and writing poetry are other effective options to help articulate burdensome thoughts and feelings. The name of the game is getting it up and out, so be creative! Paint, color, collage, draw, mosaic, sing, dance, play, listen, blog, knit, sew, crochet, weave baskets, cross stitch, sculpt, weld, carve, scrapbook, or do whatever else you feel led to do. Take a class. You don't even have to leave the house. There are webinars and online classes galore! Go ahead and look!

The internet is chock-full of creatives. We're all creative beings, and we need to find our own unique avenues for expression. Acting on your creative impulses will feel satisfying and liberating. Go crazy and create something incredible! You never know what magic it might bring!

The Spiritual Connection

Consider taking time to connect with your spirituality. What do you believe in?

There are many names for God: Jesus, The Universe, Higher Power, Supreme Being, The Divine, Nature, Source, The Higher Self, and the list goes on. Whatever name you use, I hope you know this all-knowing force is in control, so you don't have to be. It's not our job to heal the world. We can only heal ourselves, and our personal healing creates a ripple effect that can heal multitudes. Our work will affect the generations before us and after us. Don't hesitate to ask for help from above. This force is there to listen and to guide. It loves you and wants you to find happiness again. I don't believe in a punishing God, because Love cannot exist with fear. God is not out to get us or make us burn for our sins. We are all sinners by nature, and if we're warned against judging our neighbors, we also need to also stop judging ourselves.

Lean in to the Love from above (and within). It's waiting to serve you.

It isn't blaming or condemning you. That's the old paradigm, and one based on fear and control. God doesn't want to control you; He only wants to guide you back home to peace and sanity. Accept the gift. It's yours forever, no strings attached.

Gentle Movements

I know you're exhausted, so I'm not going to suggest joining a gym, pumping iron or taking up running, unless this happens to be your jam (and if it is and you have the energy, have at it). What I am going to suggest for the majority is to simply move your body every day.

Easy walking, gentle stretching, and restorative yoga are excellent ways to ground yourself, keep your energy moving, and even release pain and stuck, negative energy. You don't have to "feel the burn" for this to be effective. In fact, that might be counter-productive. We're going for gentle kindness here. We're trying to safely *return* to our bodies, so whatever form of exercise you choose needs to feel good and needn't be strenuous or used as a form of escape. Easy does it.

Learning to love ourselves again means loving *all* of us, our bodies included.

I realize this can be tough for many, and I'm going to ask you to consider this: Your poor body has been through so much. It too needs recognition and validation for all it's done for you. If you are unable to fully accept it right now, please just honor and respect it. It's gotten you this far and will be with you until the very end. It's time to make some peace with it. Be kinder to yourself and notice how much more relaxed you start to feel.

If you're able to simply walk or stretch a little every day, your stress level will decrease, and you'll be more in touch with your breath and your body. This might even help you sleep more soundly at night. If you're able, listen to positive podcasts, audiobooks, or music as you walk or talk with a friend. Remember to take pictures when you find unexpected loveliness along the way.

There's nothing that says you can't combine your exercise with nature.

Do yoga or your stretching outside. Be creative. You are part of nature anyway, so who cares what the neighbors think?

This is your time. Claim your space. Gardening can be a great option to add both nature and creativity into the mix. This can be tiring though, so take care to listen to the specific needs of your body. Again, the sky's the limit, so use your imagination and get back into your body (and always be sure to drink lots of water to keep the energy flowing).

The Healing Touch

I am a huge advocate for energy work including Reiki, Theta Healing, Craniosacral Therapy, Polarity Therapy, Somatic Release, and Myofascial Release. Sometimes we need a little extra help when energy gets stuck and/or our muscles become tight. Suicide loss *is* traumatic and just like any other trauma, this is stored within the body. When you're feeling heavy, flat, unproductive, stuck, or are experiencing nagging pain in any area of your body, reach out for professional help.

These symptoms are common when grieving, but when they can't be resolved on their own and become persistent or unbearable, it's time to do some research. Find providers who are certified and licensed in your state. Ask around and read reviews. Word of mouth is best, but always listen to your gut. If you don't like one practitioner, try another. Most energy work requires little or light touch and can sometimes be very effective even when done remotely. I wouldn't suggest this option unless you know who you're working with or know someone who does, but it's a great benefit to get work done without having to leave the house.

Myofascial Release utilizes a light touch and must be done in person by the practitioner. This therapy is wonderful for releasing muscle constrictions within the fascia surrounding the area of pain and tightness. Often, the pain is the result of past physical or emotional trauma. It might take several sessions to relieve the discomfort, but a good healer will offer you emotional guidance and helpful exercises and stretches to use in the meantime. This is a highly effective therapy when done correctly and has kept me working a physically demanding job for the last fifteen years. It's also released decades of fear and trauma which otherwise might have resulted in serious mental or physical illness down the road. Never underestimate the power of a light touch. Energy has its own rules and properties, and we don't always need to understand the details to experience deep healing. If you think energy work might be a good option for you, research it. If not, try something more conventional, like relaxation or Swedish Massage. Work within your comfort zone. Our job, as always, is to trust our own process.

I hope you understand how diligent self-care will help your mind and body to mend.

I urge you to nap, find beauty, be inspired, create, connect, and move. Ask for help when you need it, and don't be afraid to be unapologetically *you*. Remember, this journey is yours and yours alone. You are in charge, and your outcome will be a direct result of your efforts. Always choose wisely and know that you're the one to whom you need to listen.

The Safety Plan

There may be times you feel you're coming unglued and your resources are tapped.

This is normal during complicated grief. It's intense and overwhelming, even when you're taking every action possible to help yourself. People will let you down. You might let yourself down. This is to be expected. We are only human and can only take so much at any given time.

One of the kindest things you can do for yourself is to create a Safety Plan (hopefully before you reach the point of exhaustion and despair) to have if you become too overwhelmed or depleted to deal with life in general. None of this is your fault, yet you've been left to deal with the wreckage. Acknowledge this (if it's how you happen to feel) and lean on your supports. Make a list of people and places (including phone numbers) you can call to temporarily relieve you from your everyday responsibilities. This can be family, friends, church members, or neighbors. Also, keep a list of crisis lines handy (Suicide Prevention Lifeline: 800-273-8255 and Crisis Text Line: text "hello" to 741741), and make sure other household members have access to a copy of these lists as well, so they can intervene if need be. It would also be helpful to make a list of five reasons to *stay.* Come up with five valid reasons why you need to stick around when things feel unbearable and write them down. This list can include your kids, your family, your friends, your pet, your neighbor, or even a trip you've been longing to take. Seeing this list in black and white will give you a needed reality check should times get tough.

Allow your supports to pick up the slack and let go of whatever you can. (The cleaning can always wait.) Overwhelm is nothing to mess with, so honor it and speak openly about your feelings. If you're feeling hopeless or suicidal, *tell someone*. If you are for some reason unable to reach a friend, *call or text a hotline*. Hotline workers are trained to deal with people in crisis. They want you to talk and get it out. They know you're suffering, and they're trained to listen and offer support. Let them do their job and help you in any way they can. Do whatever's necessary to keep yourself safe. It's likely you need only to express these intense feelings or just need some quiet time to regroup. If you need to get away for a few days, do it. Whatever you do, understand your feelings are *normal, and don't feel guilty about them*. Everyone has a breaking point, and this is arduous work. Be gentle with yourself and honest with others. Remember, *silence can be deadly*, and at the very least, dangerous.

Keep talking and creating and follow your Safety Plan.

CHAPTER 10

Invoke the Sacred Connection

I see you... on the good days and bad
When it hurts... I am holding your hand
When it's futile... 'cause they don't understand
I hear you... when you think no one can.
If you're empty... having laid your heart bare
In the quiet... with no words left to share
When it's lonely... and no one seems to care
In this moment... I will find my way there.
I'm the message... that you see in the sky
I am rainbows... when you ask for a sign
And the sparrow... staying curiously nigh
Near the windows... peering into your life.
I am soaring... where the sky meets the sea
Out of darkness... we are finally free
I will help you... get where you're meant to be
Now be mindful... and the path will be seen.
You chose me... just as I once chose you
To learn lessons... and find our way through
It's your turn now ... to live life anew

Lean into the love … your heart – the truth.

One of the best gifts I ever received was given to me by my brother-in-law and niece, who allowed me to stay at their home the two weeks following my sister Elizabeth's death. As I sat in that quiet house day after day, surrounded by her family, plants, books, music, photos, and other personal items, I connected to her energy in a way I hadn't since we were very young. I could feel her essence everywhere: her love and her gentle, watchful spirit. There was no doubt she was present, and she was careful not to be intrusive.

Her presence was so palpable it was comforting.

She was everywhere and nowhere. We'd struggled to maintain a sisterly relationship over the years and somewhere along the way, it morphed back into the strained mother-daughter relationship from our childhood which frustrated and angered me. When I was born, she was eight years old and had to step in and act as my surrogate mother, which she notably resented. I was about nine before we established an actual friendship, but once it finally happened, this relationship quickly became the most impactful one of my young life. It strengthened me. She saw me and believed in me and, for the first time ever, I felt like someone really had my back. Strangely, this old, familiar feeling returned to me in those two weeks when I stayed at her house. Perhaps the pressure was off, and she could just be my sister again. I don't know. What I did know was nobody would ever be able to separate us again. She was closer than ever before.

One of the songs I played on repeat during those first two weeks was the old 1905 Gospel hymn, "His Eye Is on the Sparrow." (The Lauren Hill and Tanya Blount version.) I listened to it repeatedly, envisioning my sister in the arms of God and knowing, somewhere in the depths of my heart, everything was going to be okay because she was at peace. Somehow, the unbearable pain became a little more bearable knowing I could tell her anything. She was safe. I knew she could see and hear us, and I had a feeling she wanted to offer comfort and support.

When I returned home after her memorial, I noticed two birds (sparrows) looking directly into my living room window. This was not a regular occurrence, and it happened again several days later at my bedroom window. The following spring, we had baby sparrows living in the birdhouse just outside our front door, which had been vacant every year for more than ten years. The birds now visit regularly, and they always appear at poignant times: during certain songs, during visits with mutual friends, and sometimes even while I'm driving. It makes me happy knowing my sisters are still close and watching over me.

There were few things that brought me joy after Elizabeth's death, but that quiet connection, that indescribable knowing, gave me the courage I needed to keep pushing through each day. I trusted and drew strength from it, and I would soon find out I wasn't the only one receiving messages.

In the fall of 2016, I decided to join a grief support group.

There were seven of us, and we met once a week at a local church. I loved this group, and the women in it were kind and accepting. We bonded quickly and spoke openly about our grief journeys and our lost loved ones. I spoke about the way my sisters made me feel safe, and how I used to climb into bed with them when I had nightmares as a young child. I explained how strangely lost and terrified I felt without them, and how I often curled up with a pillow and cried myself to sleep at night.

At one of our last meetings, a lady named Margaret gave me a gift bag.

She said it was "something small" and asked me to open it up when I got home. When I did, I was stunned. It was a single flannel pillowcase with little Holly Hobbies all over it. The note said, "When I saw this soft Holly Hobbie fabric, I thought of you and your sisters. Hope snuggling with the pillowcase brings you a bit of comfort. Yes, you can soak it up with tears! – Margaret" She had no idea I'd recently searched Holly Hobbie on Google, or that I got a Holly Hobbie card and plaque from Elizabeth one year as a birthday gift. Someone told her, though, and she heard the message loud and clear.

Make no mistake; our loved ones are always with us even though we don't see them.

Come as You Are

I believe our loved ones want to communicate with us and, the more we expect to find their signs, the more often they will reveal themselves.

I realize not everyone believes in this sort of thing, and that's okay too; to each his own. Personally, I'm happier and more at peace knowing I'm not doing any of this alone anymore, so I ask for signs and I ask for them often.

I believe death to be the ultimate illusion.

While we'll all eventually lose our physical bodies, our souls (or our energy) will live on regardless. This explains why, even after years of separation, I feel so close to my sisters now. You can practice tapping into your loved one's energy too and, just like every other practice, it will become easier with time, patience, and a little bit of effort.

Know, too, you can connect with them no matter where you are on the emotional scale. They understand your grief and *they* can handle the truth. They're already aware of your pain anyway, so why not call on *them* to help you through it? I'd venture to guess that if you saw some signs for yourself, you'd feel a little relief and a lot more hopeful about your future. So, why not give it a go?

It isn't necessary to do anything special to meet with your loved one, although you can if you wish. Some people like to create a meeting space, either in their homes or in their minds. Whatever you choose is fine, if it feels genuine and real for you. The only requirements are your presence, honesty, and a little patience. The replies won't always come when or how we expect them (although they might) and the trick is to stay open enough to receive them. This can be tough when you're anxious or expect your message to arrive in a specific way. Letting go of the outcome is the hardest part of this process.

You'll know your sign when you see it. It will surprise you (in a good way) and it will be very meaningful. Your loved one will respond in a way you'd typically expect, according to their unique personality.

As you know, Elizabeth often speaks to me through nature. She was a quiet person and loved spending time outdoors, so this makes perfect sense. She was also a poet and sent many messages through song lyrics written by artists like James Taylor and Cat Stevens, who we often listened to together when we were younger. Think about your common interests and experiences. Do the same things you once did together and notice what happens. Even if you don't feel anything different right away, you'll feel the comfort of remembering those precious hours spent together. This can feel overwhelming or even scary at first but, don't forget, feeling these intense feelings will *not* destroy you. *They will heal you.* Creating this connection will become a vital piece of your healing process, and you'll eventually look forward to these precious moments.

Messages in the Sky

My client, Ann Marie, lost her mother early one dreary December morning. It had been drizzling, and the fog was so thick on her way home from the funeral home she could barely see to drive.

She ended up following a plumbing truck all the way home (which is ironic having come from a family of plumbers) and she managed, thankfully, to get there safely. She took her dog outside that evening, and as they walked in the yard she looked up and asked, "Mom, are you there?" A shooting star raced across the sky. Stunned, she asked, "Mom, was that you?" Immediately, and from the opposite direction, another shooting star sailed by. (Even the dog took notice.) Ann Marie then asked, "Mom, are you okay?" One more shooting star grazed the night sky (this time from the other direction). Do you think this is coincidental? I certainly don't, and Ann Marie doesn't either. She also periodically smells her mother's perfume. I'm not surprised because they were very close. Ann Marie spent a considerable amount of at the nursing home after her mother's stroke to advocate, get her to her appointments, and spend time with her.

I love these stories. They're proof that even death can't stop Love.

Say Anything

Once again, I want to remind you not to hold anything back from your loved one.

You won't be struck down for speaking your truth, whatever it may be. God isn't waiting to punish you for being angry or even enraged with your loved one. This is totally normal and to be expected. They took their leave without asking permission or saying good-bye. They left unanswered questions and more pain than we're sometimes able to effectively handle. Their decision changed our lives. *Say it like it is.* Get it all out. You owe it to yourself, your well-being, and your loved one. It's just another way to express your love.

I was relieved to finally be able to tell my sisters how I felt about them, their deaths, and my disappointments in our relationships. I'm aware they have their own disappointments too, but nothing needs to hold us back anymore. We can have the relationships we want right now, if we only ask.

Nobody in the world understands your connection as you and your loved one do.

Nobody else needs to. Guard this love with your life. It's your gift and it belongs to you and you alone. Claim it. Defend it. Honor it. Build on it. It will comfort you in ways unimaginable. It won't remove the pain, but it will give you hope, strength, and courage to face another day knowing that someone really does have your back.

The Conscious Connection

Schedule regular times to meet with your loved one.

Rekindle your common interests. Listen to your favorite music or include them in your meditation practice. Send them love, ask them questions, and ask for guidance. They want to help and support you. Taking conscious action will also help to ease your loneliness and anxiety. Just knowing they can hear you can be a huge comfort. Try it and see what happens.

Their response will depend on their unique communication style.

Was your loved one a trickster? They'll probably be up to their usual pranks. Were they thoughtful and quiet? Their response will reflect their gentle nature. Expect the expected. Who were they and how did they relate to you? Some people hear messages and others see them. Anything and everything is possible, you just need to pay attention.

My sister Suzanne has a playful spirit and doesn't communicate much with words.

She wasn't a quiet person, but when it came to her feelings, she was very reserved. For a long time, I believed she wasn't allowed to talk with me because when she appeared in my dreams she didn't speak. She only nodded, smiled, and hugged me. During one of my energy sessions she revealed she didn't have as much to say as Elizabeth and I do.

Elizabeth and I were more into words, poetry, and written expression. Sue liked to express by *doing:* dancing, decorating, cooking, and baking. She was such a lover of life, and I can feel her when I listen to certain music or when there's a family celebration of any kind. She never misses a good party, and she knows how to have a good time.

Keep Them Alive

Be sure to celebrate birthdays and anniversaries.

Just because they're gone physically doesn't mean they aren't with you. They are still very much a part of you and always will be. They already live in your heart and your mind anyway, so celebrating them will only make you and them feel more alive.

Create a special birthday or anniversary ritual.

Take the day off and visit your favorite places. Sing them happy birthday. (My sisters sing to me every year, one in each ear, according to an intuitive friend of mine.) Light a candle and eat some cake. Write them a card. Play some party music and dance around your living room. Do whatever you would've done together and do it wholeheartedly. Celebrate their life. Celebrate *your* life, and know they were a big part of making you who you are today. That alone is enough reason to throw a party! I realize it may take some time to get to this point but, when you're ready, go crazy and enjoy yourselves!

Ask for Guidance

Our loved ones want to help us, so don't be afraid to ask.

If you're having a rough go, reach out to them for help. They can see more from their side than we can, so why not? I often get the message not to take myself so seriously and to trust the natural flow. As a noted control freak, this shouldn't surprise me, and I sometimes find myself giggling about things that used to stress me out. Don't get me wrong, I still get upset and try to control, but I notice more quickly how the act of surrender brings me more of what I need. This has been a big lesson for me, and one Elizabeth sends often. (She was *very* serious, and this sometimes caused more suffering.)

I do my best to stay open to this guidance and, when I do, I'm never misled. I want you to understand that you're not alone. I know you essentially must feel and go through this anguish alone, but please remember that help is never far away. Your tears are counted, and your cries are heard. Your relationship can be anything you want it to be now, *without* the complications. Take a chance and accept this incredible gift. Your loved one is waiting to hear from you. Ask for help and watch for the signs. They will sometimes take your breath away.

Letter Writing Exercise

Write your loved one a letter and leave *nothing out.*

Tell them about your shattered dreams and the mess they left behind. Tell them what you wish you could've said but never did. Tell them about your guilt and who you blame for their death. Tell them what they mean to you and how you never got to say good-bye. Tell them about your anger and your fears. Yell at them if you need to, but say it all, the good, the bad, and the ugly. If this takes more than one writing session, so be it, but get it all on paper. After it's written, read it out loud to your loved one. They (and you) need to hear you say it. Once you've read your letter aloud, let it go. Consider it a sacred offering and burn it, tear it up, or shred it. You and your feelings matter, and I can't stress enough the importance of honoring them. This is an intense exercise, so please take extra care to comfort yourself with rest, quiet, and lots of water. You are so much more than a survivor. You are a Love warrior.

The Love Collection

This exercise is helpful for connecting to the energy of your loved one through clarity and creativity. It's always good to set an intention before you begin the project. Read through the instructions before you begin so you can be clear about your intention.

You'll need:

- 12 x 12 poster board
- 10 magazines of various types
- Elmer's rubber cement
- Scissors
- A photo of your loved one
- Optional: glitter, gel pens, colored markers, embellishments

Spend some time in meditation to connect to the energy of your loved one. You can use meditation music or connect silently. Either sit up with your spine straight or lay flat on your back. Close your eyes and put one hand over your heart and one on your belly. Follow the natural rhythm of your breath as you begin to relax. When you're relaxed enough to feel yourself "floating," concentrate on your loved one. What comes to mind when you think of them? What did you do together? Who were they to you and what was your relationship like? What would you like to be different about your relationship? How do they communicate with you? What do they say? What would you like to say to them? Do you need help with something specific? What is your intention for this project? (How would you like to be different after this experience?)

When you have a clear vision, open your eyes. Write down anything that came to mind during your meditation. (This can be words, a vision, colors, etc. It doesn't have to be a narrative.)

Begin flipping through your magazines and tear out words or pictures that coincide with what came up for you. Tear out anything applicable to your relationship or anything that brings up happy feelings of love and contentment. If you find an answer to a specific question, or anything that appears as a specific message, tear that out too. Resist the urge to cut or paste anything now. Just make a messy pile of pages.

When you feel you have enough items, begin to sort. If something doesn't feel right, eliminate it. If you're sure about it, cut it out and save it. Set items to one side until you're finished. Go back and get more images if needed and repeat the process.

When you have enough images, it's time to arrange them.

Place your loved one's picture in the center and arrange your words and pictures around it in any way that feels good to you. When you're happy with your layout, go ahead and start pasting.

Use markers or pens to add any missing words or phrases and embellish as desired.

Hang your collection in a place you'll see it often. You may now easily connect to the energy of your loved one whenever needed.

CHAPTER 11

Navigate the New

"For a seed to achieve its greatest expression, it must come completely undone. The shell cracks, its insides come out and everything changes. To someone who doesn't understand growth, it would look like total destruction."
— Cynthia Occelli

I can't begin to imagine your personal struggles, but I can recall in vivid detail how difficult it was to function in the world again following my suicide loss. I felt raw, exposed, and vulnerable to everything and everyone that surrounded me. I was a walking nerve and had to protect myself against anything and anyone who might enter and further weigh down my energetic field. I was moving in slow motion, lugging an additional 150 pounds of despair with me everywhere I went, and I couldn't afford to add any more weight to my back or I might break. I could barely tolerate being in public, and I had no energy to partake in the usual social banter. Emotionally, I was stripped bare. Broken. I couldn't pretend to be okay if I tried, and this turned out to be a life-changer for me because I learned to be alright with whomever I had to be at the time. I didn't push myself to do more than I could, and I didn't present a false persona. I couldn't, because I simply didn't have the extra energy required to pretend.

Let's face it, pretending is *work*, and living to please and pacify others will only bring on feelings of deep resentment. Pretending isn't something you can afford to do, because your own life and sanity are on the line now. It's going to take all the strength and energy you can muster to withstand the grief waves and handle your everyday responsibilities. It's time to get real about who you really want to be and what you want to allow into your life going forward.

Who Are You, Anyway?

You are stuck in limbo right now, caught somewhere between your old life and the new. This can be both exciting and troubling. You might consider trying things you hadn't previously and, while you might be thrilled, others might suddenly take offense. Some might become confused or act as though they no longer recognize you anymore because "you're not the same" and they're probably right. You're *not* the person they once knew, but this isn't a bad thing. You couldn't help but change. Your entire world changed when your loved one died to suicide, and the life you once knew suddenly came to a screeching halt. Those who haven't been where you are may not understand, and *it isn't your job to make them under-*

stand. Your job is to keep breathing, do whatever is needed to get through the day, and guard your broken heart until it becomes easier. Then, you can take on a little more each day as your body allows.

This can be a good time to get clear about any changes you'd like to make in your life, your surroundings, and in yourself. When a loved one dies, we can lose our sense of identity. This is a normal conundrum for grief survivors, as it often hurts too much to continue living the same way we did when our loved ones were here with us. There are too many triggers and reminders, so it often becomes a priority to establish new surroundings and even, to some extent, try on new identities to figure out who we want to be. Why not turn our worlds into what we truly desire? Why not try new things and new ideas instead of staying stuck in the old roles, activities, or attitudes that no longer align with who we're becoming? We can do this slowly, one small change at a time.

Grab a notebook and pen and think back to when you were young.

Write down the answers to the following questions as clearly and completely as possible:

What were your hopes and dreams as a child? What were your creative endeavors? What have you dreamt about doing or having? Is there anything you haven't done that you wish you had? What about your relationships? Are you happy with those? What would you change if you could? What would you really like to be doing for work? For fun? What are the things that normally bring you joy? When was the last time you did any of those things? When was the last time you laughed? Is there anything you have a burning desire to do? What would your ideal life look like? Who would be in it? What would you be wearing and eating? What would you look like and how would you carry yourself? How would you fill your days? Where would you live? How would you feel? Describe your home. Describe your ideal self. Describe your relationships. Describe your ideal work situation. What in your life do you want less of, or what do you never want to experience again (besides physical death, because that's inevitable)? What would you like more of? Be as specific and detailed as possible with your responses and *take your time.* These are important questions. Get to know yourself again or, possibly, for the very first time.

Change Everything

Since you can no longer return to the way things were, it's time to start working on what will soon be. I'm not talking about making major changes now. I won't ask you to sell your house or quit your job (although those might be options for the near future). I don't want you more overwhelmed than you already are. Begin with little things, and the first of these can be a list of what you know you *don't* want anymore. This will become the most important list you'll ever write because these new standards will redefine you and keep you focused forward. Keep this list short, at no more than ten items. Make these statements clear and concise and take time to seriously consider what isn't serving you. Here are some examples:

- I will no longer settle for relationships that drain me
- I will not focus on my mistakes
- I will stop feeling guilty (Yes, this is a *decision*. We weren't created victims.)
- I won't let my fear hold me back from my life
- I won't let others define me
- I will stop judging myself
- I will stop stuffing my feelings
- I will stop blaming others

Now, take these same statements and turn them around into declarations or "I am" statements.

This is really empowering and will remind you that you alone are the owner of your life, including your experiences. This might be the first time you take complete ownership of yourself. Believe me, you won't regret this decision. Take it seriously and make it count. Here are some possible turnarounds:

- I am honored and loved
- I am perfectly imperfect
- I am forgiven
- I am scared but I'm doing it anyway
- I am an original
- I belong
- I'm allowed to have feelings and to take up space
- I am responsible for my own happiness

Can you feel the ownership in these new statements? They feel so much more empowering than the initial ones, and they'll help to affirm who you truly are.

Keep this list where you will see it every day. Keep one in your car, in your purse, and on your desk. It's our job to ensure our own well-being. If we leave this job to others, we become powerless, thereby subjecting ourselves to a lifetime of perceived rejection and disappointment. People haven't really been rejecting us, *we've been rejecting ourselves*. People are simply knee deep in their own stuff and their own lives and don't always have the foresight, strength, or wherewithal to reaffirm *us*. They're too busy trying to reaffirm *themselves*. Skip the middleman and do this for yourself. You are truly the one you've been waiting for. Stop resisting and lean in. Now is the *best* time.

What else would you like to change?

The colors on the walls? Your furniture? Your hair? Does your bedroom need rearranging? Do it! Do whatever moves you and makes you feel better in your skin and in your home. Do what makes you feel more like *yourself*. If people decide you've lost your mind, let them keep their opinions, and don't worry about it. This isn't their journey, it's yours. What they think of you is none of your business. Stay in your own business and you'll be just fine.

Slow and Steady

Now that you're stepping into the new you, there will be times you feel uncertain, unsteady, and downright scared.

Don't worry, because you're in good company. I nearly panicked every time I had to leave the house to do the grocery shopping. I didn't want to run into anyone I knew or be put in the uncomfortable spot of manufacturing small talk when I could barely complete a sentence. (That was a very real thing for a while, and I was beginning to think I was stroking out or brain damaged.) I found a way to get around my fear by doing the necessary shopping early in the morning or later at night when fewer people were out and about. When I did run into people, I made the interactions as short as possible. Do what you need to, and keep in mind this will get easier as time passes, and the pain has a chance to loosen its grip. The important thing is to take tiny steps forward *with the fear,* so you don't become a hostage to it.

You might be tempted to hide to stay safe, and this will serve you for a time, but eventually, you're going to have to ease back into the world again. This will probably happen naturally, and be sure to remind yourself it's alright to do this on your own terms. It's perfectly okay to retreat to your safe space following these outings, but please don't fall into the trap of buying into every fear story your brain attempts to manufacture. Remember, its fears are only stories (not truths) and your brain is only trying to keep you safe. It will be on constant lookout to prove its current stance and, believe me, it will seem undeniably convincing. Sometimes you'll have to kindly remind your brain that *you're still in charge* and everything is going to be alright. Even if you don't totally buy this notion, it's good to say it to yourself (out loud whenever possible).

You'll begin to believe it as you take consistent action.

Small, consistent steps can lead to big results. Plus, the changes will be more prone to stick. This is brain rewiring we're doing here, and it takes practice. Go easy on yourself and concentrate on one small action at a time. You're learning how to trust yourself again and, this time, you have a lot more tools to work with. There's no right or wrong, if you keep moving *forward*. If you get stuck, it might be because you had unreasonable expectations or you're being too hard on yourself.

Imperfect Perfection

"Grief doesn't change you, it reveals you."
– John Green

Learn to be okay with imperfection. Perfection's an outlandish expectation anyway and impossible to achieve. It's our *imperfections* that make us unique and lovable. What do you remember most about your loved one? Their perfection or their humanity? In all honesty, we tend to be much more attracted to people we can *relate to,* not the ones who appear untouchable and appear to have everything together. Give yourself some grace and lower your expectations.

Choose to be thrilled with everyday accomplishments and become impressed with your innate ability to keep going. You are a warrior, after all, and you are the creator of your new life rules. You've got this, so any step, especially any new step, is really a giant leap. Challenge yourself to show up as you, in all your imperfect perfection. If you make a mistake or disappoint yourself (or someone else) accept it and move on. Don't relive it, examine it, or even discuss it. Trust you'll do better next time because you will. You've already decided, and that's half the battle. I've lightened up a lot, and this very action created the space I needed to take some big risks. I hid for too many years because I didn't want to show up imperfectly. I was finished before I ever started. No wonder I always felt paralyzed and stuck! Once I accepted my imperfections, doors started opening. I proved I could do anything I set my mind to, and I *did it all imperfectly.*

This truth really did set me free.

Your Vision

"What you seek is seeking you."
– Rumi

Now that you know what you want and know you can show up authentically, it's time to create a new vision. This is the fun part, because change can happen very quickly when you're ready for it. You already have a vision and you're taking sustained action. All you need now is a little more clarity to bring it all together. It's time to create a vision board. This will be a visual aid to inspire and motivate you to stay focused on the life you really want. You'll be amazed by how easily you'll attract what you desire.

Here's what you'll need:

- Poster board (black or white)
- At least 10 magazines of various types
- Elmer's rubber cement
- Scissors
- A favorite photo of yourself
- Embellishments (glitter glue, colored markers, colored paper for backing, stickers, etc.)

Follow the instructions given in the Love Collection Exercise, only this time concentrate on your new life. What comes to mind when you think about it? What does it look like? Who are you with and what are your relationships like? Where are you living and what are you doing for work? How are you carrying yourself? What words best describe you? What are you doing for fun? What would you like to be, do, and have? What is your intention for this project? (How would you like to be different after your vision board is created?) Collect, sort, and paste your pictures. (Don't forget to place your picture in the middle!) Embellish as desired.

Hang your vision board someplace place you'll see it often (the back of a door, your office, or even a closet can be good choices). Imagine yourself living the life of your dreams. Allow the positive feelings into your body and connect to the possibilities that await you.

The final step is to take right action, so be sure to follow the signs. Be true to your heart and follow your gut. Above all else, have faith in yourself and your own abilities.

Nothing can hold you back now unless you consciously or unconsciously allow it. Let go of any resistance or attachment to the outcomes. What is meant to be will be. Trust the process, and happy manifesting! Your new life is waiting!

CHAPTER 12

Going Forward in Faith

"How lucky I am to have something that makes saying goodbye so hard."
— Winnie the Pooh

Limitations and Other Lies

I f I could only use one phrase to sum up what I've learned from this horrible, awful, and exquisitely beautiful grief experience it would be this: We are limitless.

I don't think I would've ever *considered* this concept had my sisters not revealed it to me themselves. The Truth has proven, time after time, that even death refuses to silence the soul. It's become crystal clear to me that when someone on the other side wants to be seen or heard, they will find a way to make it happen. The soul will look for openings, in people and in opportunities, to release their message. They won't be silenced because they aren't really gone. I, for one, am grateful to be on the receiving end of these invaluable messages. I've learned I don't have to rely on my own understanding any-more – and this is a relief – because I couldn't understand it if I tried.

Something much greater than me is in control, and I'm more than happy to sit beside it in the passenger seat. There are no worries here, only wide-eyed, childlike wonder.

I have no clue why some people die violently, and others slip away in their sleep. I only know for sure that if they're no longer here, it must've been their time to go.

Why do some people survive full-on suicide attempts, while other attempters don't? I can only guess that it wasn't their time. There's no rhyme or reason to any of this and argu-ing that someone shouldn't have died (because they died to suicide) only causes people more misery than they deserve. *We* don't possess the power to save anyone who doesn't want to be saved, and there's no way for us to know when some-one's time here on Earth has run out. That is God's business. I only know reality itself doesn't lie, and as Byron Katie so eloquently says, *"Reality is always kinder than our thoughts."* I'm believing this more every day.

I could spend the rest of my life asking "why," spend my days fruitlessly fighting reality, or attempt to rescue every-one who suffers. Of course, I'll do whatever I can to educate, advocate, and support others who struggle due to trauma and mental illness, but the dark truth is, I couldn't save my own sisters. The real lesson is to learn to love each other while we're still here without the old expectations and judgments we've absorbed along the way. Why not start by learning to love ourselves? Let's stop believing the lies that we're unworthy, and let's just stop "fighting" altogether.

We can't be clear and level-headed while we're clenching our fists and defending our stance. We must drop our guard and stop resisting to become approachable. Let's focus instead on love, acceptance, and *inclusion*. Maybe then we'll find some lasting peace and finally begin to forgive ourselves.

There's No Getting Over You

I no longer believe in accidents or coincidence.

Again, *reality always rules* (you can argue with it, but it won't change), and this truth doesn't automatically make your pain or your "why" questions magically disappear.

It also doesn't mean you're not entitled to your feelings. It simply means that, in the end, everything has a reason and a purpose. We might not yet know what those reasons are, but there's always a bigger plan in the works.

I often wonder if my sisters died because they could somehow support us better from the other side. I know it doesn't make sense from here but, in all honesty, there's an awful lot that doesn't seem to add up on this planet. Oftentimes, even the most difficult situations reveal some sort of purpose after some time has passed. I don't believe our suffering goes unnoticed and I know there is purpose somewhere within our pain. Just knowing you could offer a little bit of hope to another human might be enough reason to get you out of bed in the morning. Our stories matter, and your love story might be the fuel that keeps someone else moving forward. You just never know.

Even though years have passed, I still miss my sisters.

I always will, especially when something big happens within my family, or it's a birthday or holiday. That's just the way it's going to be.

I still include them in my celebrations, but I don't ever expect to "get over" missing them. I don't have to, and why should I? There's no way to get over love. It stays with you wherever you go. I consider this love a gift, because I was lucky enough to have found it in the first place. It makes me a more compassionate person, and it helps me remember to be grateful.

I really am the lucky one.

I was able to stay and see Suzanne's kids grow up and have kids of their own. I was able to attend my nieces' beach weddings and meet their spouses. I got to hold my great-nephew, and I'm hoping to someday soon hold and hug the other three. I'm still here and I'm grateful every day for another chance to make something new happen. It's all one big experiment, and I'm finally having some fun with it because I'm not doing any of this alone anymore. I never really was; I was just asleep. You're waking up, too, to another chance at life. Make it count and go do some stuff!

Letting Go

There will come a day when you realize you haven't cried in a while, or that you haven't spent as much time thinking about your loved one. Perhaps you noticed the change of season didn't rattle you as it once did, or maybe you laughed out loud for the first time in months. These are all signs that you're healing. Don't fear you'll forget your loved one or that this means you've become callous or no longer care. *Moving past pain is a good thing, and never something to feel guilty about.* You deserve relief and happiness. You still have a life to live so, please, go ahead and *live* it! Your loved one is with you and cheering you on!

The Gratitude Exercise

This is a good time to start focusing on what you're grateful for.

Coming up with a list of five things each morning will set a positive tone for your day and keep your mind focused on what's working in your life.

We have so much to be grateful for and little reminders can give us a huge boost. I notice when depression slips in that I tend to lose sight of what's working and, instead, fix my gaze on what isn't. This is obviously counterintuitive, but I don't always catch it right away. My default was set to "never enough" for a long time. It took a considerable amount of effort to shift my mindset to gratitude but, when I finally did, I noticed I always ended up with more things to be grateful for. This is one of the best kept secrets to happy living, and it's a relatively easy habit to start. Anyone can come up with five things to be grateful for and, if you can't, you might need to find a good therapist because there could be deeper issues at play. A few things to be grateful for:

- The sunshine
- Thunderstorms
- Your health
- Your family
- Your friends
- Your pet
- Your home
- Nature
- Love
- Music
- Memories
- The kindness of a stranger
- Your life
- Your job
- Your sanity
- Your resilience
- Your courage

To intensify this practice, get your senses involved.

Feel the warmth of the sunshine on your face and let it soothe and comfort you. Listen to the sound of the rain on the grass and the soft rumbles of thunder as you imagine yourself curled up with a blanket and coffee on the sofa. Feel the love these sensations bring you. Enjoy the energetic charge you receive when you're connected to your gratitude. This is called raising your energetic vibration and you can do this whenever you need a lift, some love, or even a small attitude adjustment. A little gratitude will go a very long way.

Forgiveness and Stuff

I hope by now you're able to consider death as a new beginning, rather than an ultimate end. This idea will provide endless possibilities for gratitude, joy, and contentment. If you haven't already, I hope you can soon forgive yourself, for all you have done and haven't done, and for all you've said and left unsaid.

Nobody's perfect, and it's never too late to change your game plan or make things right again. Life is all about second, third, and fourth chances. Don't be afraid to take them and, most of all, don't be afraid of *yourself*. There's an exquisite human in there, and one who deserves your undivided time and attention. You've been through so much.

It's time to show yourself some love. Let's give it a try.

The Love Letter Exercise

I want you to write a love letter to yourself.

I know, I know … it sounds hokey but do it anyway. I first did this in my "Succulent Wild Life" class led by SARK with a bunch of other women. I thought the exercise seemed a little over-the-top at first, but after we did it as a group and people had a chance to share their letters, I was moved and inspired by the messages I heard. Suddenly, it seemed like a good thing to do, and I was excited to find out what wisdom my "Inner Wise Self" would reveal to me. I've saved my love letters and always enjoy re-reading them. I'm certain you will too.

Don't hold back. Set a timer for five minutes and make the letter as over-the-top as you like. Don't think about it or plan it. Just write whatever pops into your mind. Feel free to do this exercise whenever you need encouragement or guidance. You're sure to uncover some unexpected jewels!

I wrote the following love letter to myself on January 1st, 2017:

My Dearest Jade,

I know you are hurting deeply and it feels as though you are alone and misunderstood.

You need to know that I am always here with you, guiding you, and leading the way.

Don't worry that you can't trust yourself. You are now awake and have brand new eyes. You have become an observer, so you will be able to discern, with accuracy, what will work for you and what won't.

You are strong – never underestimate that – it has gotten you far. You are still in the game, after all. I admire your spunk and tenacity to move forward, even when you think there's no strength left.

Try not to fear what others think and say. Most of it is nonsense and indicative of where they're at on their own journey.

Always remember to view reactions as clues – watch and listen, but let it bounce off you silently, so that they will be hit by their own truth. You don't ever have to engage. Your witness and gentle silence and/ or blessing is enough.

You are doing your work well, and you don't even know it.

Embrace your emotions as friends. Get to know them. They want to be seen and heard.

When they have been honored and properly acknowledged, they will move through you easily.

I will never leave you, and I deeply respect your journey.

It has been a difficult and heart-wrenching year and a half, and you are exhausted.

There have been many changes, inside and out, that your body has not quite integrated yet – and that's okay. Give yourself permission to slow down, be still, and just observe.

The way will become clear. Be patient.

Keep reaching out and trying new (fun) things. It's good to be playful.

You need some fun. The kids need to see you play.

You are seen in your struggle, my beloved, by many.

You are not behind. Let yourself feel and express your feelings about the losses.

It's all a result of the magnitude of your love, and the greatest gift you can give.

Don't allow yourself to get snared by people who want to take you backward or hold you back. You are done with that journey. Focus only on what you want now.

That's where your happiness is. Get closer to the ones you love – they are patiently waiting.

Remember, I am always here, and you can trust the voice.

It never lies because it loves you. Always.

In Awe and Amazement –

Your Wise Inner Self

P.S. Happy New Year!

CHAPTER 13

Bumps in the Road

I want you to know you can do this.

You *can* survive this impossible grief and find happiness again. This process won't be quick, and recovery most definitely won't be linear. You might have a few good days then suddenly find yourself devastated or fearful again. *This is normal.* Always be patient with yourself and follow the specific needs of your body. Be aware, too, that when you're physically exhausted, your brain will try to manufacture all sorts of scary stories in a desperate attempt to keep you safe from the world. While these thoughts will be convincing, they are *not the truth*. Remember you are the captain of your life and you get to decide what you want to believe. *Time is precious and so are you. Choose wisely.*

Depression

It can be easy to fall into periods of depression while grieving, and it might be difficult to distinguish one experience from the other; however, if your affect becomes flat or you notice a general sense of apathy about life in general, this is a clear sign that the grieving process has been interrupted. Depression often results when we feel unable to express our feelings in a genuine way. This can happen if we tend to negate or minimize our feelings, are shamed or criticized by others for expressing our feelings, or are surrounded by people unable to hold space for us (either at work or at home). When a person receives repeated messages that her feelings don't count (or worse, that they shouldn't exist) she begins to feel invisible and, therefore, unworthy. This was a common theme throughout my own life, until I realized I could stop minimizing my own pain and validate myself. If, for some reason, you're unable to do this, *please find yourself a good therapist.* They can help you find the underlying cause of your depression and help you work through it. There is no shame in asking for additional help throughout the grieving process. I did. It will only help you understand yourself better and that is the name of the game.

PTSD

Since suicide death is often violent, it's not uncommon for suicide loss survivors to end up deeply traumatized. This, coupled with the stigma that often accompanies suicide death, is the perfect recipe for chronic, pervasive anxiety and fear. How are you supposed to feel okay again in a society that can't or *doesn't want to* understand what you've been through? (Many simply can't wrap their heads around it. I wish we had that luxury.) How do you deal with the flashbacks, agitation, and ongoing nightmares? Once again, if these symptoms become unmanageable, find a good *trauma* therapist. Know ahead of time that *not all counselors are specifically trained to handle trauma.* Look for counselors who specialize in helping people with PTSD. It might not be a bad idea to see your physician or a psychiatrist if you find you need medical intervention during this time. There is no shame in taking medication when needed, especially if it will help to restore a sense of balance in your body. I know many are against this and, personally, I've struggled with it myself. I decided, though, that my quality of life was more important than the stigma surrounding taking psychiatric medication. Say what you will, but there's a reason I'm still here and I certainly didn't do it all myself. Nobody can.

Suicidal Thoughts / Self-Harm

I know I've touched on this already, but it bears repeating: There will be times it hurts to breathe. You might even forget how to breathe. You might lose your way or periodically get trapped under the heaviness of your agony. Know this is temporary. It won't always be this intense and this all-consuming. You need time and a lot of space to come to terms with your suicide loss. Give yourself grace. Give yourself love. Above all else, give yourself permission to *feel it all*, even the desperation. I know many people who considered suicide an option following the suicide death of their loved one. How can that possibly be after bearing witness to the destruction suicide left for *them*? Didn't they already know the horror that would result from *their* death? Yes. They did, and they also felt lost, desperate, and totally alone. Like their lost loved one, they only wanted an end to their torment and to feel connected again. That's all.

Again, these feelings are common amongst survivors and are never *to be taken lightly.* If you feel this way, tell someone. Say the words out loud and talk about it. The simple act of getting the words out into the open will often be enough to diffuse the intensity of these feelings and give you a sense of relief. If nobody is readily available to talk to, call the Suicide Prevention Lifeline (800-273-8255) or the Crisis Text Line (text "hello" to 741741). Both lines are available 24/7. I've used both and the people on the other end do a good job of listening and providing resources when needed.

If you need immediate medical attention or intervention, call 911. Your safety is nothing to mess with. Always take these thoughts seriously because, as a suicide loss survivor, you are now at greater risk. You probably won't require hospitalization to get through this (although you might), but you'll have to be diligent about keeping up with your self-care practices as discussed in Chapter 9. Either way, it will all be okay. The important thing is to be certain of your safety.

As you know, guilt and blame are frequent disruptors following suicide loss, and they can become powerful adversaries to the healing process if they aren't properly addressed. It's imperative to deal with these feelings head-on to effectively move past them and, until you do, you might be prone to self-punishing behaviors.

You might try to eat, drink, gamble, or drug these feelings away, or you might look to other outside things to numb them. Besides the obvious self-harm practices, also be aware of other destructive habits such as: spending money you don't have on things you don't want or need, lashing out at others, throwing things, participating in passive-aggressive behaviors, isolating yourself, cutting or picking at yourself, disordered eating (starving yourself or bingeing and purging), pulling out your hair, engaging in dangerous sexual activity (having unprotected sex or sex with someone you just met), or banging your head against a wall.

If any of these behaviors become recurrent or pervasive, you will likely need to consult a professional to get them under control. As always, awareness is key. Keep a mindful watch over yourself and be careful not to judge. We all have our vices and our default behaviors. Forgive yourself and keep moving forward. Tomorrow is another day to begin again. Forgiving yourself first will naturally lead to the forgiveness of others.

Insomnia

Besides my physical exhaustion, nothing was more debilitating to me than the chronic insomnia. I couldn't sleep through the night and the more tired I became, the more sleep eluded me. For me, it became easier to sleep in the daytime, so I napped as often as possible, but I'm aware that's not always an option. I usually recommend cutting back on caffeine and adding chamomile tea and exercise during bouts of insomnia. However, when you're in the throes of complicated grief, the anxiety and exhaustion are so intense that these measures might avail you next to nothing.

The most effective cure for insomnia is … you guessed it … rest. Take it as easy as you can. Ask for help. Now is the right time. Asking for and accepting help doesn't make you a lesser human. It makes you a stronger and more resilient one, and it's a good practice. We aren't meant to do any of this alone. We were created to serve one another.

This is the time to count on those precious few supports you've assembled. Let them do the heavy lifting for a while and *support you*. Be sure you're regularly expressing and sharing those feelings too. If you keep them inside, they'll want to resurface when you need to sleep. Do yourself a favor and follow the prompts of your Inner Healer. She'll nudge you when she knows you need to talk, and she'll always tell you what to say. You never need to worry … just follow her lead.

If your lack of sleep is taking a toll on your memory, your ability to function, or your sanity, pay a visit to your doctor. Get some relief. A good night's sleep will help you to heal. Don't suffer when there's help available to you. There are no rewards for playing martyr. Those days are in the past. Empower yourself and take the lead. You know exactly what *your* body needs.

Isolation

While it's helpful to have long stretches of solitude as you heal, it can be easy to fall into the trap of fear and social avoidance. Suicide is frightening and learning to trust that the world can feel safe again might take a fair amount of time. Venturing out after loss is scary and it can be tempting to hide instead. I hid for decades.

The problem is, if you don't take risks, you'll never discover your true happiness.

Nobody *really* wants to be invisible or to be held back. It isn't our natural state of being.

We want to be free and expansive and, to do this, it means being uncomfortable sometimes. It's how we grow and evolve. This is tough after loss, but it isn't impossible, especially if someone has your back. When you surround yourself with people who understand and "get you," they will lead by example. You'll know you're not the only one being real and vulnerable in this world. Your people will cheer you on when you succeed, and they'll pick up your pieces when you fall. (If you don't stumble along the way, you're not really stepping out. You're playing it safe. This is fine, but you won't find out what you're really made of until you show up authentically, as you, in all your glorious goofiness.) The right people will be okay with you and everything you are (and aren't).

They won't have a secret agenda, and they will encourage your exploration and growth.

If you find yourself being avoidant, it's helpful to introduce positive self-talk and affirmations. We all need a little encouragement from time to time, and who better to encourage you than you? Tell yourself what you need to hear. Scared to go to the store? Tell yourself, "I've got this. I have a right to take up space." If attending a work outing is making you nervous, tell yourself, "I can do this. My presence matters." Lift yourself up. You get to decide which voices you wish to heed. Just know that chronic isolation will lead to loneliness, stagnation, and, ultimately, depression. Personally, I can't afford to go there anymore. I now know who I am so there's too much work to do.

My days of staying small are over. Life has been patiently waiting for me, and it's waiting for you to join too.

Triggers

A trigger is a strong emotional response to a sight, smell, or sound.

Triggers are specifically linked to PTSD survivors, but anyone who's experienced a frightening event (or a difficult loss) can also experience triggers. They are unpredictable and very distressing. One minute you're having lunch at your favorite restaurant and, within seconds, you're frozen and breathless after hearing a car backfire in the parking lot. The sound transports you back to the trauma, and you're helpless to speak, move, or respond.

This, too, is the pattern of grief. We get periodic respites, but it's never long before the next tsunami hits, forcing us right back into the desperate reality of our loss. Managing these storms is difficult because of their unpredictability. You can be okay one day, and completely out of commission the next, without any warning. Grief will get your attention whether you're ready or not, so it's best to respect it, and follow its lead. Don't expect to make sense of this because grief has its own rules. You can count on one thing for sure, though, grief always has your best interests in mind. It knows what you need, and it'll keep showing up until you honor it. There's no way around this (believe me, I've tried everything). You will be triggered, and you will be reminded to look at and deal with things you'd rather deny. Nobody said this would be easy. I wish we didn't have to go through this, but the only way out is through. The sooner you can get real, the faster you'll start to heal.

This, I know, you can count on.

Get What You Need

If, at any time on this journey, you feel as though you need professional support, get it.

There is no good reason *not* to help yourself. There is plenty of support available, if you're willing to seek it. People are willing and waiting to support you, and again, sometimes those people aren't your immediate friends and family. Keep in mind your family members will find their own unique way through this journey, so they might not be available to help you on yours. Don't hold this against them, because they're hurting too. Empower yourself and trust you'll be led to the right supports. You most definitely will. Ask God, your Inner Healer, and your loved ones for guidance.

The universe will have your back if you remain your greatest advocate.

CONCLUSION

Never Again Alone

Y ou're never alone.

Though the road you're traveling is rocky and unpredictable, you will always be supported and loved. The gift of grief is yours to embrace and cherish. It won't always feel good, but this is the unspoken truth about love: It doesn't always come in the familiar shapes of rainbows and little pink hearts. Perhaps the purest forms of love look more like total annihilation; the painful sobs, the swollen eyes, the wails of desperation ... these are love in disguise and are the rarest of all gifts. Honor them with your life. You trusted yourself and another human being so much, the pain of their absence nearly killed you. Nearly – but you're still here. You're here to tell your love story.

I thank you for giving me the chance to tell mine.

You now have the tools you need to embrace your own unique experience.

Always remember that your way is the right way, if you're following the direction and prompts of your body. Surround yourself with people who accept you, and your intense emotions, without judgment. *Be* the person who accepts you, and your intense feelings, without judgment. Remember that grieving takes a significant amount of time, and there are no prizes waiting for those who "finish" first. Know what you need. Trust yourself and know your higher power and your loved one(s) have your back.

Your space, your time, and your energy are sacred.

Respect your needs, honor yourself, and expect to be your biggest advocate. Give yourself a break. Surround yourself with beauty and avoid negative media and people because toxic energy spreads like wildfire. Remember that silence can be deadly, so let it all out in the safest way possible. Quiet time will help you integrate and heal.

Remember that all feelings are normal and necessary.

You must feel to heal. Feelings always pass, so hang on tight, and do your best to accept them. If you're ever in crisis or need someone to talk to in the middle of the night, call the Suicide Prevention Lifeline (800-273-8255) or the Crisis Text Line (text "hello" to 741741).

Partake in bodacious self-care practices.

If you don't do it, nobody else will. Express yourself in creative ways and be inspired. Solicit help from your family and friends and accept this help with grace and humility. It's good for the soul, and one day you'll be able to return the favor when they are in need.

Never underestimate the power of the healing touch.

Connect with your lost loved one.

Death doesn't kill a relationship, it only alters it. Let your loved one live on in your heart and mind and speak with them often. Ask for support and watch for signs that look, feel, or sound like them. The best gifts come at unexpected times.

Be yourself. It's the best way to be.

You are here for a specific reason, so step into your power. Decide what you want and what you don't want. This is your life and your experience. Create the life you really want because you deserve to be happy and whole.

Don't expect to get over your loss.

You don't get over love and you wouldn't want to anyway. Integration is the real goal. Remember there is always a plan, and a heart of gratitude will create more to be grateful for. Trust and you will surely receive.

Be aware of complications.

Mindfully watch over yourself and be on the lookout for stuck energy and complacency. Get professional help from a doctor or trained therapist when you need it. If you're feeling suicidal, call the National Suicide Lifeline (800-273-8255) or the Crisis Text Line (text "hello" to 741741). Follow your gut and *care* for yourself. Research your caregivers and choose wisely.

I wish you unbridled joy and complete healing.

I long to see every suicide loss survivor living the life of their dreams while surrounded by limitless love and abundance. We've been through so much despair. Now is the time to reclaim our place in the world. We deserve so much more than a mere existence. We deserve to *thrive*. We aren't here to play small. We're here to live large and with reckless abandon, like kids. It took me nearly fifty years to accept myself and, now that I have, I can't imagine anyone I'd rather be. I always knew exactly what I needed, but I resisted my own wild and unconventional ways. I stifled myself and cut off my own air supply in the process. Maybe losing my sisters forced me to finally make peace with me. I don't know. I do know I'll never leave me again. Call me crazy, but I've never been more content in my entire life. I'm pretty sure my sisters prefer it that way. My healing has affected everyone around me, including them.

I had lots of help, and there's plenty of help available for you too. Reach for it. The world needs your presence and your voice, now more than ever. You belong. We all do.

Acknowledgments

This book would not have been possible without the support of my kids. Kim, Tanner, Hannah and Jack: Your love keeps me grounded and focused on being a better human. You love me unconditionally, hold me to high standards, and never give up on me (even when I've given up on myself). I hit the jackpot with every one of you. You have hearts of gold and your mother's stubbornness. (Yikes and thank God!) For all of this and so much more, I am eternally grateful. Thank you for believing in me. I love you more than you'll ever know.

To my sisters, Suzanne and Elizabeth, for leading me home. I wouldn't have survived without you. Sue, I'll spend the rest of my life learning to love as generously and whole-heartedly as you did. Elizabeth, I promise to be courageous for all of us. (I'll go kicking and screaming sometimes, but I'll show up as myself: gloriously goofy. You can laugh... I can take it now.)

For my nephew and nieces: Thank you for keeping me in the loop. It's my honor to witness each one of you moving forward in courage and in grace. You have no idea how proud I am of the people you are. You represent your mothers with great love, and I'm privileged to watch as your lives unfold. Truly, I am the lucky one.

To Adrienne Betts, my bestie and my soul sister: I'll never forget all you've done for me and my family. You're the one I prayed for as a kid: my one true friend until the end. I love you with all my heart. Thanks for being sublimely you.

To the counselors and healers who supported my awakening: Mary Yahle, Kelly VanVliet (RIH), Mary Ann Moller-Gunderson, Nancy Early, Katherine Skrzypek, Jillian Versweyveld, Evie Schulz, and Diane Burns. Without guidance and support from other strong women, I might not be here today. Thank you for showing up, as yourselves, to walk beside a wounded human while immersed in your own difficulties/pain at the same time. It takes great strength to hold space for others, and each one of you is a bona fide Love warrior. I'll never be able to fully express the depth of my gratitude for your generosity, patience, and genuineness.

Thank you to the angels who inspired me while they were here and now support me from above: Heather McKeen, Shannon Watson, Meryl Brusser, and Charlotte Schroeder. Our time together was way too short, but you touched my heart deeply and changed the way I look at myself and the world. I'm thankful to have you on my team and look forward to seeing you again on the other side.

Thanks to Peter Jackel for making this book "ours," and for the stories that make me smile when life gets hard. You're a loyal friend and generous to a freaking fault. Your kindness will never be forgotten. To you, I lob a resounding FOB!

To my chosen family (of clients, teachers, and cohorts): Thank you for your relentless encouragement, kind words, and for taking me as I am, no matter what. You guys are the best!

Special thanks to my editors: Cynthia Kane and Anna Paradox for reading and re-reading until your eyeballs fell out! I'm eternally grateful for your input!

To my coaches (in order of appearance): Susan Ariel Rainbow Kennedy, John Kim, Virginia L'Bassi, Melissa Drake, and Angela Lauria: Without your belief in my abilities and your tireless support, this book might never have been written! Thanks for leading the way and believing in me. I'm proud to be amongst such inspirational way-showers!

To the Morgan James Publishing team: Special thanks to David Hancock, CEO & Founder for believing in me and my message. To my Author Relations Manager, Bonnie Rauch, thanks for making the process seamless and easy. Many more thanks to everyone else, but especially Jim Howard, Bethany Marshall, and Nickcole Watkins.

Lastly, I want to thank you, dear reader, for taking a chance on *yourself.*

You trusted your instincts to find your way here and out of total despair. You are courageous, my friend, and much stronger than you know. We can make a difference here, by choosing to *stay*. Even when it hurts. One minute at a time. One breath at a time. You've got this, and you know I've got you.

Thank You!

Thank you for taking the time to read *Wake Me from the Nightmare: Hope, Healing, and Empowerment After Suicide Loss.*

I hope I've offered some useful tools to make your grief journey a little smoother. Remember to have solid supports in place as you continue to navigate this unpredictable terrain.

Since your grief will be ongoing, I want you to know I've still got you covered.

I've created a companion video series that goes with this book to further support your success. You can sign up for it at: www.noparameters.org/thank-you.html

Be well and be encouraged. You are seen and dearly loved.

About the Author

R. Jade McAuliffe is a certified life coach trained by The
Angry Therapist.

After three family tragedies,
Jade awakened from decades
of self-avoidance, self-loath-
ing, and self-sabotage. The
agony of losing her last living
sister to suicide left only

enough energy to deal with her grief. She knew she had to
face her pain head-on or risk losing herself for good.

By listening intently to her own inner voice, she began to
heal and finally to live in an authentic way. On her quest for
self-love and support, she discovered life coaching and began
investing in her own well-being and success. For the very first
time in her life, she learned to embrace her entire story.

In 2016, Jade joined her local Suicide Prevention Education and Awareness Coalition and, as co-chair of the 2017
Walworth County "Out of the Darkness" Community Walk

for suicide prevention and awareness, she spoke publicly about her personal experience with lifelong depression, PTSD, suicidality, and suicide loss.

You can find her stories, poetry, and art on her Blog Page at: www.noparameters.org. Her work has also been featured on Elephant Journal and The Good Men Project. She hopes these stories will offer strength and hope to other trauma and suicide loss survivors, so they can learn to trust themselves and the world again.

Jade's life has been devoted to helping herself and others overcome fear, limitations, and heartache.

She is the Mid-Western version of the girl next door.

Resources

National Suicide Prevention Lifeline: 1-800-273-8255
  (available 24 hours a day, 7 days a week)
Crisis Text Line: Text "hello" to: 741741
  (available 24/7)
The Trevor Project: 1-866-488-7386
  (LGBTQ support available 24/7)
Veterans Crisis Line: 1-800-273-8255 and press 1.
  (available 24/7 You can also send a text to: 838255)
Spanish Speaking Crisis Counselors: 1-888-628-9454
American Foundation for Suicide Prevention (AFSP) Resources:
  https://afsp.org/find-support/resources/
International Association for Suicide Prevention (IASP) Resources:
  https://www.iasp.info/resources/Crisis_Centres/

Printed in the USA
CPSIA information can be obtained
at www.ICGtesting.com
JSHW082337140824
68134JS00020B/1721